WHO HAS SEEN THE WIND?

Who has seen the wind?
Neither you nor I.
But when the trees bow down their heads
The wind is passing by.
                    ROBERT LOUIS STEVENSON

When the Holy Spirit is present somewhere
there is bound to be *a wind*
because he is the living God
who re-creates the face of the earth.
This re-creation of the face of the earth
means a great movement
which brings fresh air
into the life of mankind and of the Church.
The wind of Pentecost does not destroy life:
it makes the gift of life more abundant—
with more movement.
If there is no movement at all in a place
it is not likely that the Spirit of God . . .
is present there.
                    LADISLAS M. ÖRSY, S.J.
                    The Lord of Confusion

Who Has Seen The Wind?

THE HOLY SPIRIT IN THE CHURCH AND WORLD

Louis M. Savary, S.J.

The Regina Press • New York

1976
THE REGINA PRESS
7 Midland Avenue
Hicksville, New York 11801

Library of Congress Catalog Number: 75–26026
ISBN 0–88271–029–x

Cover photo by Joseph Vesely

Manufactured in the United States of America

CONTENTS

INTRODUCTION

It was Pope John XXIII who spoke so convincingly about the "signs of the times" among which he recognized the Holy Spirit at work revealing to the Church the direction it should follow in the ever new task of offering God's redemption and salvation to all peoples. Perhaps the most striking sign of the times is this rediscovery of the Holy Spirit, experienced as powerfully alive and at work in the Church and in the world.

The Church is and was always seen as "a creation of the Holy Spirit." Brought into existence and kept continuously alive by the Spirit, it is the same Spirit that constantly renews the Church in both its outward manifestations (structure) and inner form (spirit). One cannot deny that today we are experiencing a much deeper awareness of the Spirit's presence among us both individually and in community. Indeed what has come clearly into focus is the fact that the Church is first of all a "charismatic community," i.e. an entity that is based entirely on the gifts which the Spirit distributes to each individual within the community and to the community as a whole. Not only is the hierarchical structure given for the well-being of the community (Church) but each member is endowed with a gift or gifts (charism) which must be exercised if the redemptive task of the community (Church) is to be fulfilled.

Vatican II clearly recognized the charismatic structure of the Church as well as the necessity of exercising the individual gifts received from the Spirit. "It is not only through the sacraments and Church ministries that the same Holy Spirit sanctifies and leads the People of God

and enriches it with virtues. Allotting His gifts 'to everyone according as he will' (I Cor. 12:11), He distributes
special graces among the faithful of every rank" (*Consti-
tution on the Church*, no. 12).

The discovery and proper use of the charisms given to
individual members of a community seems to be the way
in which the Spirit wants to renew the Church today. One
might call this a renewal from within. Groups exist in the
Church which once again recognize and experience the
gifts of the Spirit. These gifts urge them to renew their
personal lives as well as the life of the community in
which they live. It is equally true that these charismatic
communities can serve as agents of renewal only if they
work within the context of the larger community of the
faithful, the Church. Let no one "extinguish the Spirit,
but test all things and hold fast to that which is good"
(See: I Th 5:12, 19–21).

REV. THOMAS A. KROSNICKI, S.V.D.
Associate Director
Bishops' Committee on the Liturgy

One

WHO IS THE SPIRIT?

$\mathcal{W}$ITH BODY, MIND AND HEART

A HUNGER FOR GOD

In the world today there is a great hunger for God.

It is a *felt* hunger. It will not be satisfied by intellectual discussions, logical arguments, or authoritative teaching. It will not be satisfied by doctrinal books or scholarly lectures.

People hunger for God himself. They want to experience him, to feel him inside themselves, to sense his presence around themselves, to be in touch with his vibrant power.

Spiritual hunger will be satisfied only by religious experience that involves bodies, emotions, minds, and hearts.

People want to *know* God, in the fullest human meaning of the word "know."

WITH BODY, MIND, AND FEELINGS

In Latin, there are at least two different words for our English word "know." One is *scio,* from which we get

3

words like "science" and "omniscient." *Scio* means "I know with my mind."

A second Latin word for "know" is *sentio,* from which we get words like "sensitive" or "sense." *Sentio* means "I know with my feelings, with my body, and with my senses."

Believers today, unsatisfied with religious experience that involves merely knowing with their minds, would like their prayer to involve bodies, emotions, and hearts as well.

Unsatisfied spiritual hunger shows itself in younger people. Brought up in traditional Christian churches, many young people are seeking new spiritual meaning in teachings and disciplines of the East. Some explore Buddhism, Taoism or Sufism. Others commit themselves to Zen, Yoga, Hare Krishna, or other ways of life unfamiliar to most of us.

Why do young people seem to find Eastern traditions attractive? Why do they leave their Christian churches? One reason is that the Eastern approaches provide experience that involves body, mind, and heart. Gurus and spiritual masters offer transcendent experience that asks for response from the whole person, not merely the mind.

Of course, Christian spiritual experience can be a total personal experience. From the church's earliest days, Christian experience was meant to be a total personal involvement, in which physical actions and feelings played a major part.

Unfortunately for many Christians today, religious experience probably means little more than reciting sterile prayers memorized in childhood, or sitting bored through a weekly ritual event labeled a "Sunday worship service."

If this is all that Christianity can offer, it is no wonder young people go off in search of more excitement and involvement on other religious paths!

Yet, Christian religious experience can be exciting and involving. It can be a total personal experience, if it is open to the influence of God's Spirit, if it is viewed as "falling in love" with God and creation.

A TOTAL RESPONSE

Think how people come to know and love each other. It probably begins with an emotional awareness or a feeling response. Perhaps their hearts beat a bit faster, or maybe they feel a sense of peace when they see each other.

Notice how often people use the feeling word "like," when talking about those they love. "I like her," they may say, or "I like the way she talks," or "I like to be with her."

Notice, too, how many "feeling" and "sensory" words they tend to use in describing friends. They can be "warm," "close," "strong," "loving," "tender," and so on. It's almost impossible to avoid "feeling" words when talking about personal love experience.

Although personal relationships are not based on "pure feeling" or "mere emotion," feelings and emotions form a critically important part of all friendships—even friendships with God and creation.

LOVE AND FAITH

When people feel love toward someone, they don't say "My mind finds you acceptable." They say, "I love you." Love involves a personal commitment. It requires a total personal response—body, mind, and heart. So, when people really say, "I love you," to someone, a total person is speaking, a commitment is being made.

Faith, like love, involves a total personal commitment. When people make an act of faith, they say, "I believe you . . ." Faith involves something beyond mere intellectual assent. A true believer says more than, "I understand this doctrine . . ."

A faith affirmation, "I believe you . . .", involving commitment to another person, might bring about changes in the believer's behavior, feelings, thoughts, and interests.

To say, "I understand this doctrine . . ." merely offers intellectual assent to a *sentence.* It indicates that the mind is doing its job of processing ideas. As for heart and feelings, they could well be off on some other planet.

Sentences in a book or a newspaper may be satisfied simply with a mind response, but persons—including God—expect a personal, feeling response.

When people find themselves responding to God without feeling or other personal involvement, but with only their minds, they may be just reacting to a "theological sentence."

In religious experience, people can learn to let themselves respond with everything that is them—body, mind, and heart. They can allow themselves to involve their feelings in responding to God. Helping religious response become a total personal experience is the work of the Holy Spirit.

Deep in everyone's heart the Spirit waits. Those open to his spark will feel their religious experience like a flame, an on-fire love experience.

"Come, Holy Spirit," cries the church in her liturgy, "and enkindle in us the fire of your divine love."

2

ⲁS A CHILD

PICTURE HIM

For most Christians growing up, the Spirit was not an important figure in their church life.

When today's grownups were children, going to church was probably enjoyable enough. The pastor may have talked a lot about heaven and it made everyone feel good, so people came back the following Sunday to hear more nice things.

Some decades ago, children probably learned that heaven was a kingdom where a lot of holy and important personalities lived. God the Father, they were told, was king there, and Jesus his Son sat next to him.

There was a third very important person called the Holy Spirit (people said "Holy Ghost" then), but people were never able to picture him, and children could never figure out where he sat in heaven.

Grownups said the Holy Spirit had appeared on earth, at times looking like tongues of fire, at times looking like a white dove. Since children then probably couldn't imagine why a divine person would want to appear this way, many never thought much about the Spirit.

RECALLING CHILDHOOD

One young man recalled his childhood religious experiences, and how little the Holy Spirit was involved in them:

Much more attractive to my young mind and feelings were the saints. They lived in heaven, too. First came Mary the mother of Jesus, and Joseph her husband. I had books in which Mary and Joseph were pictured. Next, most vividly I recall St. Ann who was Mary's mother, and St. Stephen who was patron saint of our church.

All these people in heaven were colorful figures in my mind. Together with God the Father and Jesus, I knew stories about each of them, and would tell those stories to anyone who wanted to hear them. I enjoyed strong feelings of love for all my saint friends, often prayed to them, and hoped one day to meet them walking along the streets of heaven.

Among all heavenly inhabitants, the Holy Spirit seemed least involved in this man's life as a child. While he had no difficulty accepting the Spirit as a divine person, it never occurred to him to pray to the Spirit, as he seemed to have done most fervently to the Father, to Jesus, Mary, Joseph, and the other Saints.

THE YOUNG MAN CONTINUED HIS REFLECTION:

Nor can I remember my parents, my family, or our pastor speaking about the Holy Spirit with much excitement. Of course, we mentioned his name every time we made the sign of the cross, and we affirmed our belief in him whenever we recited the Apostles' Creed. But otherwise, hardly anyone talked about the Spirit, except on two days, Pentecost Sunday and Confirmation Day.

SPECIAL SPIRIT DAYS

On a special Sunday each year at church, people read the Pentecost story from the gospels. Children would remember imagining the Apostles hiding fearfully in an upstairs room in Jerusalem. Then suddenly tongues of fire hung from the ceiling above their heads. After the tongues appeared, the Apostles weren't afraid anymore. Jesus had sent the Fire to them, children were told. The Fire was really the Holy Spirit.

Confirmation Day was the other time when the Holy Spirit was important at church. In keeping with Christian tradition, children were taught to believe he would come down to strengthen those who were receiving the sacrament of confirmation that day. When the Spirit came he would make them strong and brave soldier-Christians. They would be willing to suffer and endure difficult things for Christ.

After confirmation, young believers probably imagined the Spirit returning to heaven to await the next group of children.

A middle-aged woman shared her secret childhood thoughts about the Holy Spirit.

Each time I attended a confirmation service, I secretly hoped the tongues of fire would actually appear as they had to Jesus' disciples, hanging from the ceiling. But nothing like that ever happened.

Since there were plenty of others in heaven to whom I could

send my loving thoughts and prayers, my child's mind didn't worry much about the Holy Spirit. He could not be very important, I told myself, or I would have heard much more about him from people who were likely to know about such things.

Many Christians probably grew up as this woman did, knowing next to nothing about the Holy Spirit and his place in the lives of people and in the church.

WITHOUT RECOGNIZING THE SPIRIT

Until recently, seminary training differed very little from church life in awareness of the Holy Spirit. Religious students may have read a book or two about the Spirit, but many people in monasteries, convents, and seminaries never seriously encountered him or got deeply in touch with ways he was affecting their lives.

People simply did not recognize him. So, in meeting priests, ministers, or other religious people who talk about the Holy Spirit merely in theological terms—offering abstract definitions instead of personal experience—please don't blame them. Disappointingly, many of them have never really met the Spirit, or encountered him in their lives, or fallen in love with him, or been transformed by him.

WHO IS THIS SPIRIT?

Only recently in Christian churches have people, including priests, ministers and sisters, been encountering the Spirit in great numbers.

Only recently have people come to realize how powerfully the Spirit has been at work within them—though fully the Spirit has been at work within them—though many are still unaware of his influence in their lives.

Only recently have believers come to realize that the Spirit works not only in people's *minds* (teaching them), but in their *bodies* (letting them feel his power), and in their *hearts* or spirits (inviting them to commit themselves to his work).

Only recently have believers come to recognize the Spirit's crucial role in the life and growth of each church congregation.

In ever increasing numbers, people are asking, "Who is this Holy Spirit?" "What does he do?" and "Where is the best place to look for some answers about him?"

A good place to begin searching is in the Bible.

THE SPIRIT'S OWN BOOK

A BOOK BY THE SPIRIT

The Bible is really the Holy Spirit's own book.

Some people are surprised at that statement. But if you ask Christian or Jewish theologians, "Who is the true author of the Bible?" they will most likely reply, "The Holy Spirit."

From earliest Judeo-Christian history, theologians have asserted that the Holy Spirit is ultimately the author of scripture. What this means is that the books of the Old Testament and the New Testament were written under the Spirit's inner guidance. So, although humans were actually putting words and sentences on paper in their own style and in their own words, they were writing ideas the Spirit wanted them to write.

This is one reason the Bible is called *the word of God*. In reading the Bible, humans are reading the message God wants to communicate to them.

Through inspiration, the Holy Spirit is author of the Bible in such a way that the Bible is *His word*.

13

WAYS TO RESPOND

When people hear the statement, "The Bible is the Spirit's own book," they may respond in at least two ways.

First, they may respond from their intellect, saying, "I understand with my mind what you say."

Or, they may answer with a personal commitment, saying, "I also believe that the Bible is the Spirit's own book."

If they answer the first way, merely with the mind, their statement will probably have little or no feeling connected with it. But if they answer with a personal commitment, they will somehow *feel* the words they say.

Recently, a businessman eager to deepen his Christian faith agreed to try an experiment. The instructions were simple:

Take a Bible in your hand, look at it, and say, "The Holy Spirit inspired this book, and I am holding it. It contains his word for me." Then observe what happens to you.

What are your feelings? What kinds of thoughts are running through your mind? Do you want to open the Bible in your hands? Do you want to put it back on the shelf? Are you embarrassed? Are you feeling joyful, skeptical, anxious? Have you ever felt like this before?

Silently, he held the Bible in his hands for a few minutes. At first he seemed to be fighting an interior battle. Then, his face broke into a smile, and he simply said: "The book I hold in my hands can help transform me, if I want it to."

The men who wrote the Bible were transformed men. They were writing what they knew and experienced themselves.

TO BE INSPIRED

Theologians say the Bible was designed and inspired by the Holy Spirit. But how did the men who wrote it feel while they wrote? How did it feel to be inspired by the Holy Spirit?

Whenever someone or something influences people's thoughts, feelings, ideas, or actions in a special way, we say they are inspired. Generally, when people speak of being inspired, they mean that some positive outside influence is having an effect on them.

Inspiration is not an unusual event. Frequently inspiration experiences occur in daily life. For example, people might make such statements as, "Joe gave me the idea to repair the transmission this way," or "All of a sudden I felt the urge to drive over and visit you," or "When I saw that beautiful hillside, I just had to paint it," or "My high school English teacher was my incentive to become a writer."

Each of these statements describes an inspiration, a positive influence coming from outside.

Just as people might be inspired by Joe, the beautiful hillside, or an English teacher, so the biblical writers were inspired by the Spirit.

The very words inSPIRation or inSPIRed find their source in the word SPIRIT.

WHAT THE SPIRIT WANTED

To explain divine inspiration, it is not necessary to imagine that the Spirit knocked on the apostles' door and dictated what they were to write. It is enough to know that they felt impelled to share their "good news" experience in writing. What they wrote was what the Holy Spirit wanted them to write, because the very impulse to write came from the Spirit. "No prophecy ever came by the impulse of man," explained Peter the Apostle, "but men moved by the Holy Spirit spoke from God." (2 Peter 1:21)

Paul confirmed the idea when he wrote to Timothy, "All scripture is inspired by God." (2 Tim 3:16)

Many people are surprised to hear that the Bible is the Holy Spirit's own book. But even more surprising is that hardly anyone realizes that much of the Bible, especially the New Testament, is written about the Spirit. Throughout the New Testament are stories about the Spirit and the work he did and continues to do in the world, especially through Jesus.

JESUS AND THE SPIRIT

The Holy Spirit plays a key role in many significant events of Jesus' life. The Spirit is present when Mary conceives Jesus. "It is by the Holy Spirit that she has conceived this child," said the angel of the Lord to Joseph, according to Matthew.

At the beginning of Jesus' public life, he received the Spirit. When Jesus stood before John the Baptist in the River Jordan, he was energized by the Holy Spirit appearing in the form of a dove.

Throughout Jesus' ministry, the Spirit remained with him. Jesus reports healing the sick and casting out evil spirits by the power of the Holy Spirit.

At the end of his life, Jesus promised to send the Spirit to help the apostles complete the mission he had begun.

"He will instruct you in everything," said Jesus, "and remind you of all that I told you." (John 14:26)

When Jesus left his disciples and returned to his Father, the Spirit became the source of power and brotherhood among the early Christians. "They were filled with the Holy Spirit and continued to speak God's word with confidence." (Acts 4:31)

A STARTLING FACT

Some theologians assert that the Holy Spirit is perhaps the major character in the New Testament.

Recently, Reverend Morton T. Kelsey took the time to count biblical verses where the Spirit is mentioned or where the Spirit's work is described (healing, prophecying, and the like).

Kelsey found that practically half—47 percent—of the entire New Testament is about the Holy Spirit.

This is a startling statistic considering how little the Holy Spirit is spoken of from pulpits in Christian churches throughout the world today.

Few can say that 47% of the sermons they heard were about the Holy Spirit. The Holy Spirit seems to have a much lower percentage of interest in many Christians' lives.

A SPECIAL GROUP OF BELIEVERS

But the tide is turning. The Holy Spirit is being rediscovered. His importance in human life is being recognized by certain believers.

This rediscovery is due in a very special way to a growing group of believers who speak of themselves as *pentecostal* or *charismatic* Christians—both Catholics and Protestants.

They call themselves *pentecostal* because central to their religious experience is the felt presence of the Holy Spirit among them. They explain that, even though they don't see fiery tongues on the ceiling, they feel the Spirit's presence in their gatherings much as the Apostles felt his presence on Pentecost day.

They call themselves *charismatic* because they emphasize in their worship and daily life special gifts *(charismata)* of the Spirit, such as healing, teaching, prophecying, speaking in tongues, doing kindnesses, and so on.

More than all other believers in our own day, charismatic Christians count on Christ's promise, "I will send the Spirit." (See John 15:26)

FINDING HIM IN THE BIBLE

Charismatic Christians discover the Spirit and learn to recognize his presence by studying the Bible, the Spirit's own book.

Taught how to interpret their own experience by the scriptural books, they discovered that Christ had indeed sent the Spirit into their own lives. Christ had always been sending the Spirit, they learned, even though at first they did not know how to recognize him. "You know him," said Jesus, "for he dwells with you, and will be in you." (John 14:17)

Becoming sensitive to the ways the Spirit works, charismatics learned to welcome the Spirit into their lives.

They met the Spirit and in many ways were transformed by him. He became their teacher. "He will guide you into all the truth," said Jesus. (John 16:13)

In the gospel according to John, Jesus explains to the disciples how the three divine persons in the Trinity relate to each other. He tells them,

If you love me, you will keep my commandments. And I will pray the Father, and he will give you another Counselor, to be with you forever. (John 14:15–16)

The Counselor to whom Jesus refers is the Holy Spirit, who will replace Jesus as the apostles' teacher. The Spirit will interpret Jesus' teachings and will reveal whatever they need to know.

The Holy Spirit, whom the Father will send in my name, will teach you all things, and bring to your remembrance all that I have said to you. (John 14:26)

He will guide you into all truth . . . and he will declare to you the things that are to come. (John 16:13)

Jesus sees the Holy Spirit and the apostles working side by side preaching the "good news," being witnesses to Jesus' message throughout the world.

The Spirit of truth . . . will bear witness to me; and you are also witnesses, because you have been with me from the beginning. (John 15:26–27) He will glorify me for he will take what is mine and declare it to you. (John 16:14)

In Jesus' mind, the Spirit is very important. His tasks involve carrying on the work Jesus began, giving strength and knowledge to the apostles, and being the source of life to the young Christian community.

4

I CALL YOU FRIENDS

FATHER, SON AND SPIRIT

In the beginning, God the Father was uttering his Word. That Word so completely expressed the Father's divine nature that the Father's Word may be called his Son. The Word who is Son is just as much God as the Father is, and just as much a person as the Father is.

These two divine beings, Father and Son, lovingly relate to each other.

Wherever two beings lovingly relate to each other, whether they be humans or divine persons, there arises a third reality—something that is distinct from either of them, yet needs both to become real. This third reality is "their relationship."

When two humans are friends, "their relationship" forms a new reality which we call their friendship.

Similarly, the love between the Father and the Son— "Their Relationship"—describes the Holy Spirit, a third divine reality.

RELATIONSHIP—A NEW REALITY

Some may find it difficult to think of a relationship as a new reality, a new being. But there are many common personal relationships that people treat as new realities.

For example, when two people join together in marriage, their relationship forms a new personal reality. Husband and wife are sometimes treated as separate individuals. At other times, people deal with them precisely as a marriage relationship, for example, as a new reality that can own possessions, incur bills, enjoy sexual privileges, have children, and so forth. While the marriage relationship involves both partners, yet it is somehow different from either of them.

In a similar way, a group of people join together to form a corporation. The corporation becomes a new legal person in the world, and enjoys a life of its own, with its own liabilities, obligations, and capacities. A corporation has life and can grow. It has a birthdate and can die, without the individual stockholders having to grow or die.

A family is another relationship that has its own identity, independent of individual family members. The Cabot family's life and history began before any of those living today, and its own future will probably continue long after those living today have died. Outsiders can relate to a family, and not to any particular individual member. People speak of the Smiths as likeable people, while they find the Adams family very reserved.

Chemical relationships also are good examples of relationships that create new realities. Molecules of hydrogen and oxygen, distinctly different chemical elements, combine in a certain way to produce water. Water is a third reality, different from hydrogen or oxygen, yet totally dependent upon both.

LOVE CREATES A PERSON

Marriages, corporations, families, and chemical compounds all share one thing in common—they are new realities formed by relationships.

In a similar way, theologians view the loving relationship between the Father and the Son as a new reality.

The love of God the Father for the Son and the Son's love for the Father create a friendship bond. This loving relationship is so complete that the divine friendship is itself a new personal reality. The Holy Spirit may be described as the friendship between the Father and the Son.

At the River Cardoner, Ignatius Loyola, founder of the Jesuits, enjoyed a mystical experience. He had a vision of the keyboard on a church organ. Ignatius claimed that he learned more about the Trinity in this momentary experience than he had learned in all his years of theological study.

Without having a mystical experience, people may profit from Ignatius' vision by performing an experiment on an ordinary piano or organ.

First, play two different notes, one at a time. Notice how each note has a clear identity.

Next, play the same two notes simultaneously, and notice the *new sound.* Musicians call notes played together a chord.

The new sound is a *relationship,* with a musical identity all its own, different from either of the notes played alone.

Think of God the Father as a single divine love note on the piano, and the Son as another single divine love note. In this case, the Holy Spirit is the *new sound* that occurs when the two notes are played together forming a divine love relationship.

THE SAME SPIRIT

Since the Holy Spirit is the love relationship between Father and Son, he belongs both to the Father and the Son.

The Bible sometimes refers to the Holy Spirit as the "Spirit of God" or the "Spirit of Jesus." Both expressions describe the same Spirit. The Father refers to "my Spirit" and Jesus refers to "my Spirit" in much the same way that either a husband or wife might refer to their relationship as "my marriage" or "my love."

The Holy Spirit is identified as the current of love flowing between the divine persons. In fact, wherever the Spirit is, people will find sharing, encounter, interaction, love relationships, friendships with God.

So too, wherever people are sharing, interacting, loving and caring, the Spirit is present.

"WE" DESCRIBES A NEW REALITY

Friends are people who experience things as a "we." Friends often describe the things they do together as shared experiences, for example, "We really enjoy vacations together," or "We think alike," or "We wouldn't like a house that large."

I can experience things as an "I" and you can experience things as "you." But if we are truly friends, *our friendship can experience things,* that is, "we" as a new reality can experience things.

More than "I"-ness or "you"-ness, friendship describes a "we"-ness.

The Holy Spirit reveals divine "we"-ness, since he is the expression of the Father's and Son's acting together as friends. Whenever the Father and Son act together, the Holy Spirit is at work.

"If a man loves me," said Jesus, "he will keep my word, and my Father will love him, and *we* will come to him and make our home with him." (John 14:23) That is, the love between the Father and Son—which is the Spirit—will live and vivify each friend of Jesus.

GOD IS FRIENDSHIP

Cassian the Abbot, one of the founders of monastic life, asserted that "God *is* friendship." When his fellow monks objected to his defining an ineffably transcendent God by such a simple human relationship as friendship, Cassian reaffirmed his statement.

"God is friendship," Cassian repeated, "and whoever lives in friendship lives in God and God lives in him." Cassian was saying that true friendship, wherever it is found, is divine by its very nature.

In his assertion, Cassian was echoing John the Evangelist's statement, "God is love, and he who abides in love abides in God, and God abides in him." (1 John 4:16)

When people experience friendship with each other, Cassian would say, they are experiencing God's Spirit, that is, they are participating in God's love relationship.

The Spirit is the atmosphere in which people breathe the life of God. The Spirit is the oxygen of divine friendship.

When people enter the Spirit or allow the Spirit to enter

them they are sharing in the love relationship between the Father and the Son.

Jesus hinted that entering a loving friendship was equivalent to entering the life he shares with the Father. "No longer do I call you servants," Jesus said to the Apostles, "but I have called you friends, for all that I heard from my Father I have made known to you." (John 15:15)

And in another place Jesus says, "By this will everyone recognize you as my disciples, if you have love for one another." (John 13:35)

Jesus uses words like "love" and "friends" to describe those who follow him. He sees his church as a community of friends. For him, it will be *friends* who make up the Kingdom. (See John 15:13–15.)

To participate in friendship is to live in the divine currents of love flowing between Father and Son. In this river moves the people of God. The Spirit permeates the church, encouraging its growth and development.

AN IMPORTANT QUESTION

What does it mean to be a human being? The way people answer that question will have a strong impact on their life.

Those who think humans are basically good will have a positive outlook, and people may tend to live up to their good expectations.

On the other hand, those who think humans are ineradicably evil, will tend to see people reflecting their worst expectations. Their lives will probably be lived in fear, discouragement, and despair.

Jesus' answer to the question, "What does it mean to be

a human being?" explodes any answer given by people before him.

While almost all views up to Jesus' time saw human beings as temporal and finite, Jesus saw everyone capable of living forever with unlimited potential.

According to Jesus, all humans are loved by God, and invited into friendship with the Father on an equal basis with the Son. This means that people are called to participate in divine life. Like Jesus, their friend and brother, they are invited to share the Trinity's own life forever, continually co-creating the universe with the Father, Son and Spirit.

"The glory which you gave me, I have given to them," said Jesus to the Father about his friends, "that they may be one even as we are one, I in them and you in me, that they may become perfectly one, so that the world may know that you sent me and *have loved them even as you have loved me.*" (John 17:22–23)

An unbelievably high calling: in the Father's eyes, to be equal to Jesus.

WHAT DO YOU HEAR?

Charismatic Christians hear Jesus addressing them as friends, as equals. They hear Jesus inviting them directly into his own divine friendship with the Father.

Charismatic Christians find their lives being transformed by the realization that God has always been embracing people in his love and inviting them into "we"-ness with him.

The classical Greek myth about Prometheus tells how people first got fire. Before fire came to earth, humans were weak, defenseless, and deprived of warmth. Fire was the symbol of divine life, and only the gods possessed it.

To help his fellow humans, Prometheus sneaked up to Mt. Olympus where gods dwelled, stole some fire, and brought it back to earth. From then on, people enjoyed its power just as the gods.

People have no need of a Prometheus to steal life and love from a jealous god. According to Jesus, they have only to let the Spirit set them aflame.

Jesus' words, taken literally, assert that the Father loves each person just as much as he loves Jesus. Deep within each person lies the fire of divine life and love waiting to be ignited by the Holy Spirit.

People, in turn, are free to "set fire" to the earth. They may turn the world on, because they participate in God's own life.

For this reason praise is a frequent prayer of charismatics who realize they are gifted with a divine fire and live in the Holy Spirit. In the psalmist's words they say, "I will praise the Lord as long as I live." (Psalm 146:2)

The Book of Psalms ends on a note of universal praise:

> Let everything that breathes
> praise the Lord!
> Praise the Lord!

5

*T*HE THIRD PERSON

MORE THAN AN IMPERSONAL FORCE

Speaking of the Holy Spirit as "divine friendship" may lead some people to think of the Spirit as a kind of impersonal force. "He is a source of life," some might say, "or primordial energy, a dynamic earth power, even a love relationship, but not a person."

But Christian believers assert that the Holy Spirit is not only a life force but is also a person.

Without denying that the Spirit may be described as the divine friendship between the Father and the Son, believers may also say that he is a person.

It is not impossible to think of a relationship also as a person. People do it whenever they talk about corporations, such as IBM, GM, AT&T, and thousands of others like them. Each corporation is precisely a set of relationships among people, and this set of relationships itself acts as a person distinct from any individual corporate stockholder. IBM, Inc., for example, can go into debt, change its purpose, introduce new ideas into its production, do business with other individuals or corporations, and so on.

Talking about a corporation as if it were an individual, people might say, "I'm going to write IBM a letter," or "I'd like to work for Sears," or "I hate GE for the bad deal it gave my father," or "MCA has produced this wonderful executive." In short, people treat corporations as persons.

Likewise, as "the divine friendship" the Holy Spirit can and does act as a person distinct from the Father and the Son.

THE SPIRIT IS A PERSON

The Bible speaks of the Spirit engaging in activity that is precisely personal. Here are at least twenty kinds of activities that show the Spirit to be a person. For these are activities only a person can perform.

1. *The Spirit prays.* "We do not know how to pray as we ought, but the Spirit himself intercedes for us with sighs too deep for words." (Romans 8:26)

2. *The Spirit makes decisions and exercises free will.* "The Spirit apportions gifts to each one individually as he wills." (1 Corinthians 12:11)

3. *The Spirit teaches.* "The Holy Spirit will teach you all things, and bring to mind all that I have said to you." (John 14:26) (See also Nehemiah 9:20)

4. *The Spirit communicates.* "The Spirit will not speak on his own authority, but whatever he hears he will speak, and will declare to you the things to come." (John 16:13)

5. *The Spirit searches.* "The Spirit searches everything, even the depths of God . . . no one comprehends the thoughts of God except the Spirit of God." (1 Cor. 2:11)

6. *The Spirit knows and understands.* "We have received the Spirit which is from God, that we might understand the gifts bestowed on us by God." (1 Cor. 2:12)

7. *The Spirit loves.* "So I appeal to you, my brothers, by our Lord Jesus Christ and by the love of the Spirit, to strive together with me in your prayers to God on my behalf." (Romans 15:30)

8. *The Spirit moves.* "In the beginning . . . the Spirit was moving over the face of the waters." (Genesis 1:2)

9. *The Spirit grieves.* "Do not grieve the Holy Spirit of God, in whom you were sealed for the day of redemption." (Ephesians 4:30)

10. *The Spirit is sensitive to the needs of others.* "The Spirit helps us in our weakness." (Romans 8:26)

11. *The Spirit baptizes.* "John baptized with water, but before many days you shall be baptized with the Holy Spirit . . . You shall receive power when the Holy Spirit has come upon you." (Acts 1:5, 8) (See also John 3:3-5)

12. *The Spirit regenerates and renews.* "God saved us . . . in virtue of his own mercy, by the washing of regeneration and renewal in the Holy Spirit." (Titus 3:5)

13. *The Spirit gives witness.* "We are witnesses to these things, and so is the Holy Spirit." (Acts 5:32)

14. *The Spirit fills people with life.* "He who believes in me," said Jesus, "as the scripture has said, 'Out of

his heart shall flow rivers of living water.' Now this he said about the Spirit, which those who believed in him were to receive." (John 7:38–39) (See also 2 Cor. 3:6 and Acts 2:4)

15. *The Spirit relates to Jesus.* "And Jesus, full of the Holy Spirit, returned from the Jordan, and was led by the Spirit for forty days in the wilderness . . ." (Luke 4:1)

16. *The Spirit takes the place of Jesus.* Jesus was the first counselor to his disciples, but at the end of his life Jesus said to them, "I will pray the Father and he will give you another counselor, to be with you forever, even the Spirit of truth . . ." (John 14:-16–17)

17. *The Spirit shows people where they are doing right and wrong.* "And when the Spirit comes, he will convince the world of sin and of righteousness and of judgment . . ." (John 16:8 ff)

18. *The Spirit accepts and rejects.* "The Holy Spirit said, 'Set apart for me Barnabas and Saul for the work to which I have called them.' " (Acts 13:2)

19. *The Spirit brings and keeps people together.* "Be eager to maintain the unity of the Spirit in the bond of peace. There is one body and one Spirit . . ." (Ephesians 4:3–4)

20. *The Spirit rejoices and brings joy.* "The kingdom of God . . . means peace and joy in the Holy Spirit." (Romans 14:17), or "You received the word . . . with joy inspired by the Holy Spirit." (1 Thess. 1:6)

In the eyes of New Testament authors, the Holy Spirit is indeed a person, distinct from the Father and the Son, who acts in ways we associate only with persons: knowing, loving, choosing, teaching, grieving, searching, sharing, communicating, praying, assisting, caring, relating, and many more.

RELATING TO THE SPIRIT AS A PERSON

Because the Spirit is a person, charismatic believers enter into relationships with the Spirit.

To establish a love bond with the Spirit is to enter into the very life of the Father and the Son. It means becoming personally involved with the Father and Son, in their own friendship with each other.

Relating to the Holy Spirit as a person carries the believer into the very heart of the Trinity.

Relating to the Spirit as a person releases to the believer all the life forces and energies at the disposal of the Spirit. In the Spirit, believers enjoy not only their own merely human powers, but, gradually, as they relate more and more deeply to the Spirit, they learn to live and act ever more completely with divine attitudes and divine energies.

By the Spirit, they are brought more fully into the life of God.

6

$\mathcal{W}$HO IS GOD?

THREE DIVINE PERSONS

The Bible applies the term "God" to three distinct divine persons—Father, Son and Holy Spirit.

Christians clearly assert their belief in the divine Trinity whenever they say the Apostles' Creed.

> We believe in one God, the Father, the Almighty . . .

> We believe in one Lord, Jesus Christ—the only Son of God, eternally begotten of the Father, God from God . . .

> We believe in the Holy Spirit, the Lord, the giver of life, who proceeds from the Father and the Son. With the Father and the Son he is worshipped and glorified.

In the Bible and in the Creed, the Holy Spirit is presented as God, and as distinct from the Father and the Son.

THE SPIRIT IN THE OLD TESTAMENT

In the Old Testament, the Holy Spirit is presented as divine. Sometimes he is referred to as the *Spirit of God.* For example, in Genesis, "In the beginning . . . the Spirit of God was moving over the face of the waters" (Genesis 1:1 RSV). Later in the same Old Testament book, Joseph is referred to as "a man endowed with the Spirit of God" (See Gen. 41:33–41).

At other times, the Holy Spirit is referred to as *a divine spirit* ("I the Lord have filled Bezalel with a divine spirit" Exodus 31:3), or as the *spirit of wisdom* ("Now, Joshua, son of Nun, was filled with the spirit of wisdom, since Moses had laid his hands upon him." Deut. 34:9).

THE SPIRIT IN THE NEW TESTAMENT

In the New Testament, the Holy Spirit is further revealed as Jesus' Spirit, too. "He will instruct you in everything," explained Jesus, "and remind you of all that I told you." (John 14:26)

In reminding them of all that Jesus told them and announcing to them the things to come, the Spirit will be expressing Jesus' knowledge. "In doing this," explained Jesus, "he will give glory to me because he will have received from me what he will announce to you." (John 16:14 NAB)

The Holy Spirit is not only Jesus' spirit but the Father's spirit as well. From this viewpoint, the Spirit will speak of what Jesus and the Father share in common. Jesus explains how this happens. "All that the Father has belongs to me. That is why I said that what he [the Spirit] will announce to you he will have from me." (John 16:15)

ALL THE DIVINE QUALITIES

Thus, the Holy Spirit possesses all the qualities of the Father and the Son.

The Spirit is present everywhere ("The spirit of the Lord fills the world." Wisdom 1:7)

The Spirit sees all things ("Where can I go from your Spirit? From your presence where can I flee?" Psalm 139:7)

The Spirit hears all things ("The Spirit of the Lord knows what man says." Wisdom 1:7)

The Spirit knows the future ("By his powerful spirit he looked into the future . . . he foretold what should be till the end of time, hidden things yet to be fulfilled." Sirach 48:24–25)

The Spirit is able to expel demons ("It is by the Spirit of God that I expel demons," said Jesus. See Matt. 12:28)

The Spirit is able to speak through people ("The Spirit of your Father will be speaking in you" Matt. 10:20, or "It will not be yourselves speaking but the Holy Spirit" Mark 13:11, or "The Holy Spirit will teach you at that moment all that should be said." Luke 12:12)

The Spirit is a divine teacher ("When the Spirit of truth comes,—he will guide you to all truth." John 16:13)

In fact, no one can enter into God's kingdom without being born again of water and Spirit. (John 3:5)

THE SPIRIT IS A DISTINCT DIVINE PERSON

Just as the Spirit possesses the divine qualities of the Father and the Son, the Spirit is also distinct from the Father and the Son. This is especially clear in the New

Testament, where the Spirit plays a distinctive role in the incarnation of the Son and in the formation of the people of God.

Mary conceived Jesus in her womb by the action of the Holy Spirit. " 'The Holy Spirit will come upon you,' the divine messenger announced to Mary, 'and the power of the Most High will overshadow you; hence, the holy offspring to be born will be called Son of God.' " (Luke 1:35) Or in Matthew's version, " 'It is by the Holy Spirit that she has conceived this child,' said the angel of the Lord to Joseph in a dream." (Matt. 1:20)

The Holy Spirit entered John the Baptist. ("He will be filled with the Holy Spirit from his mother's womb." Luke 1:15)

The three persons of the Trinity are clearly and distinctly mentioned in all four evangelists' descriptions of Jesus' baptism at the beginning of his public life.

When Jesus came to the Jordan River to be baptized by John, the Spirit descended—"in visible form," said Luke, "like a dove," said Mark—and hovered over Jesus. And bystanders heard the Father's voice "from heaven"— according to Matthew, Mark and Luke—saying, "This is my beloved Son. My favor rests on him." (See Matt. 3:13–17; Mark 1:9–11; Luke 3:21–22, and John 1:29–34.)

Distinctly, it was the Spirit who led Jesus into the desert, where he was put to the test by the devil.

SIN AGAINST THE SPIRIT

Jesus clearly distinguishes the Spirit in the matter of sin. According to Jesus, all sins, except blasphemy against the Spirit, seem to be forgiveable sins. Sins against the Son will be forgiven, explained Jesus, "but whoever says anything against the Holy Spirit will not be forgiven." (See Matt. 12:22–32.)

Whatever this special sin may be, theologians have not yet agreed. But whatever it is, it is certainly supremely serious to Jesus.

BAPTIZE IN THEIR NAMES

At the end of his life, Jesus commands the disciples to baptize people "in the name of the Father, the Son and the Holy Spirit." (See Matt. 28:16–20), once again reaffirming the fact that there are three persons, fully divine and distinct from each other.

HOW TO RECOGNIZE THE SPIRIT

According to Jesus' promises, the Holy Spirit constantly gives life to the body of believers. For this reason, say the Pentecostal Christians, believers should expect to experience the *presence* and *power* of the Holy Spirit in their own lives.

Presence refers to the Spirit's companionship, the divine person dwelling in a believer's consciousness as friend, teacher, advisor, revealer, supporter, and so on.

Power refers to the Spirit's capacity to accomplish unusual things. When the Spirit's power operates through people, they are capable of acting in extraordinary ways, performing what some people would call miracles.

Jesus' promises of presence and power were experienced by the first believers on Pentecost day and in the months and years that followed. The saga of the early Christian churches, recorded in the *Acts of the Apostles,* is a story of the presence and power of the Holy Spirit.

May people living in the twentieth century expect to have similar pentecostal experiences?

"Yes," say the Pentecostal Christians. These believers are characterized by their confident belief that Jesus has made a promise to send the Spirit and that he will be true to his promise. Jesus' words in this regard are unequivocal. His promise of the Spirit encompasses all time.

"I will ask the Father and he will give you another counselor to dwell with you forever." (John 14:16)

How can people learn to recognize the power and presence of the Spirit in their own lives? "You know him," Jesus said, "because he dwells with you and will be in you." (John 14:17)

Paul's letter to the Galatians lists the fruits of the Spirit: "love, joy, peace, patience, kindness, goodness, faithfulness, gentleness, self-control." (Gal. 5:22–23) People may examine their lives for such experiences. Whenever they are experiencing love, joy, kindness, peace, and the rest, they are experiencing the Spirit in their lives.

The Spirit, like the invisible wind, is known by his works. In the words of Robert Louis Stevenson,

> Who has seen the wind?
> Neither you nor I.
> But when the trees bow down their heads
> The wind is passing by.

Two

THE SPIRIT
IN THE CHURCH

7

*C*HURCH: ORGANIZATION AND COMMUNITY

FORMAL AND INFORMAL

The Church is both a formal organization and an informal community.

Many people may misunderstand the Church because they view it exclusively as a rigidly structured organization, or exclusively as an informal collection of all Christians. To deny either the Church's formal side or its informal side is to neglect part of its reality.

As an organization, it has rules and laws, it places people in positions of power, it deals with money and management, it generates paperwork and red tape, it enters into legal relationships, it may be efficient or inefficient, it decides who belongs to it and who may become members. In short, the Church as an organization reaps the usual crop of advantages and liabilities of any organized corporation.

The Church is also a loving community that contains many informal groups of believers. Such friendship groups are expressions of the Church whether or not they are worshipping in churches or being guided by bishops.

In the Apostles' Creed, the Church is referred to as the "communion of saints." "Saints" includes those who have chosen to follow Jesus' teaching, who have adopted his mentality, who have begun to look at the world the way he did.

When groups of such believers gather in Jesus' name, wherever they may be, they are an expression of "the Church." Or, in the words of St. Irenaeus, "Where the Spirit of God is, there is the Church and every grace."

In contrast to the formal, organization, and structured Church, The Christian community as a group of friends may be described as informal, spontaneous, and unstructured.

As an organization, the Church is formally divided and structured into hierarchies, dioceses, parishes, bishops, priests, ministers, laity, and so on.

As a community of friends, the Church is much less structured. The Spirit's activity in the human community is not limited by parish boundaries or denominations. For example, many pentecostal prayer groups include Protestants and Catholics.

The Spirit's presence among people creates the Church and continues to create it, both in its formal structure and its informal groups.

On the level of organization, the Spirit works through people within the Church structure by providing public worship and sacraments.

On the informal level, the Spirit also acts through families, prayer groups, and friends who meet in hundreds of different places for hundreds of different reasons.

MUTUAL STRENGTH

Formal and informal Church groups strengthen each other.

The formal organization provides a clear membership structure, a sense of belongingness, a collection of doctrines and teachings. It provides church buildings, ministers, and a variety of opportunities and suggestions for worship—publicly and privately.

In turn, informal friendship groups that belong to the "communion of saints" provide ways of channeling interests, bringing people together, consolidating personal energies, getting things done, initiating new ways of relating, creating new forms of worship.

For example, pentecostal groups in the Church began meeting as informal groups of friends, principally to develop new ways of praying together and of living out the ideas of Jesus in their daily lives.

Even though pentecostal groups still meet informally, they also count on the organized Church to provide many structures and supports, for example, the eucharist and other sacraments, buildings for worship, editions of the Bible for reading and study, schools for theological training.

On the other hand, the formal Church counts on enthusiastic believers to vivify its structures: to fill churches with song, to help support needy people, to attend theological schools, to make biblical principles come alive among people, and so on.

While the Church is truly an organization, it is just as truly a community of friends. Since the Spirit operates wherever people are, he operates both in the formal and informal Church.

8

*T*HE SPIRIT IN THE NEW CHURCH

I WILL SEND HIM

Jesus wished his community of friends to develop fully and spread their message throughout the world. To do this, his small group of followers, like adolescents, needed to separate from the parent's protection to fully mature. To become a Church, they needed to develop their independence under the Spirit's guidance.

Jesus is willing to leave earth in order that the Spirit may come in all fullness: "It is much better for you that I go," he said on the night before he suffered. "If I don't go, the Paraclete will not come to you, but if I go, I will send him to you." (John 16:7)

At his ascension Jesus again referred to the Spirit when he said, "I send down upon you the promise of my Father. Stay here in the city until you are clothed with power from on high." (Luke 24:49)

Both Father and Son want people to share the same Spirit and the same powers of the Spirit as they (Father and Son) do.

The Spirit is crucial to the life and growth of the new community—as crucial as he was to Jesus and his work. Remember how the Father filled Jesus with the Holy Spirit, and sent him into the world to preach reconciliation. "I will put my Spirit upon him, and he shall proclaim justice to the nations." (Isaiah 42:1)

In a similar way, Jesus in turn sent his followers into the world to preach God's mercy, giving them his Spirit.

John records Jesus' words this way: " 'As the Father has sent me, so I send you.' Then he breathed on them and said, 'Receive the Holy Spirit.' " (John 20:21–22)

POURING OUT HIS SPIRIT

God has always desired to give people his Spirit.

From Old Testament times, God has been pouring out his Spirit on the earth to make his people fully alive. "I will put my Spirit within you, and you shall live." (Ezekiel 37:14)

A few pages later in the same book, God once again asserts his promise to send the Spirit, "I will not hide my face anymore from them, when I pour out my Spirit upon the house of Israel."

God's promise of the Spirit extended beyond the house of Israel to all humanity, according to the prophet Joel,

Then afterward I will pour out my Spirit upon all mankind.
Your sons and daughters shall prophecy.
Your old men shall dream dreams.
Your young men shall see visions.
Even upon the servants and handmaids in those days,
I will pour out my Spirit. (Joel 2:28–29)

During a speech on Pentecost, Simon Peter quoted this Old Testament passage (See Acts 2:17–18) and announced that today Joel's prophecy had come true. The community of Jesus' followers who had counted on Jesus' promise "I will send the Spirit," now rejoiced to know that his promise had come true.

To the crowd marveling at the signs and wonders done by the apostles, Peter reminded them that this was the Spirit's work: "He has poured out this that you see and hear." (Acts 2:33) From the very first day, the community of believers felt the presence of the Spirit.

CLEARLY RECOGNIZED IN THE CHURCH

The Spirit's presence may be clearly recognized in the significant acts and events of the new Church.

On Pentecost day, believers were filled by the Spirit. "They were all filled with the Holy Spirit and began to speak in other tongues, as the Spirit gave them utterance." (Acts 2:4) Visitors to Jerusalem from many different countries "each heard them speaking in their own language." (Acts 2:6)

At another crucial event, when Peter and John were on trial before the Sanhedrin, "Peter, filled with the Holy Spirit, spoke up." (Acts 4:8) In court, Peter's confident voice and boldness startled the doctors of the laws when they realized that the apostles were obviously uneducated, common men.

When believers gathered to pray, they clearly felt the Spirit's presence. "The place where they gathered shook as they prayed. They were filled with the Holy Spirit and continued to speak God's word with confidence." (Acts 4:31)

When the community elected new people to speak the word of God, the new missionaries were filled with the Spirit. Stephen was one of these. "They selected Stephen, a man filled with faith and the Holy Spirit." (Acts 6:5)

When new villages accepted the "good news", the apostles prayed that people there might receive the Holy Spirit. Peter and John did this with the new believers in Samaria. Upon their arrival, the two apostles "imposed hands on them and they received the Holy Spirit." (Acts 8:17)

THE SPIRIT'S INITIATIVE

Sometimes the Spirit impelled believers to approach other people to tell them about the Lord.

The Spirit said to Philip, "Go and catch up with that carriage." Philip ran ahead, met the official riding in the carriage, and soon Philip was "telling him the good news of Jesus." (See Acts 8:26–40.)

When Peter hesitated to associate with a group of Gentiles from Caesarea, the Spirit instructed him to accompany them. Peter reported, "And the Spirit told me to go with them." (Acts 11:12)

While the apostles worked to spread Jesus' message, the Spirit continued shaping the Church in his own way. In Joppa, "the Holy Spirit descended upon all who were listening to Peter's message." (Acts 10:44) This startled the already-Christian believers, since the listeners were Gentiles. (Acts 10:45) And the Spirit prevailed.

Another time, Peter began to address a group of Gentiles and the Spirit took over. "The Holy Spirit came down upon them," explained Peter, "just as it had upon us at the beginning." (Acts 11:15) How could Peter refuse to accept as Christians those whom the Spirit marked, as clearly as if it had been another Pentecost!

Sometimes Christians reported the Spirit speaking to them. "On one occasion, while they were engaged in the liturgy of the Lord and were fasting, the Holy Spirit spoke to the group: 'Set apart Barnabas and Saul for me to do the work for which I have called them.' " (Acts 13:2)

Clearly, whether in selecting apostles, making converts, urging others to do some deed, or guiding believers in prayer, the Holy Spirit was taking charge in the new church. As promised by Jesus, the Spirit was creating and shaping the group of friends, who were known "by their love for one another." (John 13:35)

Everywhere the community was at peace, even under persecution. The community "was being built up and was making steady progress in the fear of the Lord; at the same time it enjoyed the strength of the Holy Spirit." (Acts 9:31)

9

$\mathcal{T}$HE CHURCH: ONE BODY, ONE SPIRIT

THE TOTAL CHRIST

Early Christian believers saw themselves as a unity because they all shared the same life. "The community of believers were of one heart and one mind." (Acts 4:32) They drank from the same cup of worship, they shared the same bread, they spoke the same promises to God, they lived by the precepts of the same Jesus.

"It was in one Spirit that all of us—whether Jew or Greek, slave or free—were baptized into one body." (1 Cor. 12:13)

The one body is the Christ Body. Or, since God is love, the one body is Love's Body. "There is but one body and one Spirit," asserts Paul (Eph. 4:4) There is only one body, and it is the Christ. Every human is invited to be a part of the Total Christ.

Even some fervent believers find it difficult to grasp and accept the idea of the Total Christ. Very simply, it means Jesus-plus-all-humans-throughout-history-that-he-has-taken-to-himself *as one body.*

The "one body" idea suggests perhaps the richest meanings for the word Church. As the Christ Body, the Church is seen as something beyond a structured organization and something beyond an unstructured community of friends. It becomes a gathering of everyone, from Adam and Eve to the last child that will ever be born, into one huge living organism. This will be the Total Christ —Love's Body, vivified by the Spirit of God.

"God has fashioned us for this very thing and has given us the Spirit as a guarantee of it." (2 Cor. 5:5)

The life of the Spirit is life in the Body, individually and collectively. The whole Body shares the same life.

SPIRITUAL ECOLOGY

Actually, the idea that everybody shares the same life system is not new to ecologists. For years scientists have been saying that everything on the planet is interconnected.

People are dependent, for example, on the earth's atmosphere for oxygen to breathe, on plants for vitamins, on animals for protein foods and clothing, on water to facilitate body processes, on sunlight for seeing, on natural resources for fuel and building materials, and so on.

Interdependency occurs on every level. For survival, animal needs include water, plants, sunlight, and other animals. Plants and flowers themselves need water, earth, sunlight, and insects for their survival. Everything on earth is clearly connected to everything else.

In a similar way, believers can become sensitive to ecology of the Total Christ. They can begin to see the

Church through the eyes of Jesus as one immense organism interconnected by the Spirit.

The Spirit's task is to bring about unity in this body.
"That they may be one," said Jesus in his prayer to the
Father, "as we are one, I in them and you in me, that they
may become perfectly one." (John 17:22–23)

BRINGING CHRIST ALIVE

Paul sees the work of the Spirit as bringing Christ Jesus
alive in people. "To me," said Paul, "life means Christ."
(Phil. 1:21) In other words, when people let the Spirit
totally transform them, they can affirm, "to be alive
means to be part of the Total Christ."

People need not fear ceasing to be themselves if they
allow the Spirit to dwell in them, said Paul. In the Total
Christ, people will not lose possession of their minds and
wills. They will not even lose their bodies. In fact, their
bodies will be glorified.

"If the Spirit of him who raised Jesus from the dead dwells in
you, then he who raised Christ from the dead will bring your
mortal bodies to life also through his Spirit dwelling in you."
(Rom. 8:11)

So, in numberless ways the Spirit wants to come and
dwell in people more and more fully, if only they would
invite him. There is nothing the Father and Son wish to
give people more than the Spirit. People have only to
welcome the gift of divine friendship.

In the human community, the Spirit himself wants to
transform everyone into sons and daughters of God. He

wants to come and make his home in human hearts. He is working to keep the Total Christ body healthy and growing.

THE BODY'S HEALTH

The final healthy unity of all people on earth is far from realized. Many people still go to bed poor, hungry, and sick. Others suffer from political oppression or are victims of wars. Still others are kept from a full life by ignorance and fear.

People find, too, that certain social structures tend to destroy and suppress human potential rather than develop it. Inflation, depression, unemployment, discrimination, prejudice, injustice—the list of social ills seems endless.

In all this, the Spirit is at work, in the Church and out of it, inspiring individuals and groups to use their talents and gifts. Some he calls to personal acts of caring and kindness.

Others he calls to work on larger projects: to make everyone in the Body aware of existing injustice and oppression, to mobilize large numbers of people and their power to heal, and so on.

In general, the Spirit is intent on healing the ills of the Christ Body, and looks to believers in the Church to cooperate. He elicits their concern for the whole.

The energy that will heal the Body's ills is love.

TO EXPERIENCE GOD'S LOVE

One way of describing the Spirit's purpose in the Church is to help each human, and all humans, personally experience the love between God the Father and Jesus the Son (this love is the Holy Spirit), that we "may attain to the fulness of God himself." (Eph. 3:19)

The Spirit is at work in the Church, in the humans who accept Jesus, to help them see the world the way Jesus does.

The Spirit's hope is that believers "may be able to grasp fully, with all the holy ones, the breadth and length and height and depth of Christ's love, and experience this love which surpasses all knowledge." (Eph. 3:18–19)

At work among people at this very instant, the Spirit can do immeasurably more than people ask for or imagine. The Spirit in people is involved in a process beyond their wildest dreams.

TOTALLY AND THOROUGHLY

Scriptural writers reinforce again and again the idea that God is present totally and thoroughly in people's lives.

For example, to many religious people, the temple or church was the only holy place. It was where they felt they could best get close to God.

Paul the Apostle goes further. He asserts that people are themselves the very temples where God's Spirit comes to live. "You are the temple of God and the Spirit of God dwells in you." (1 Cor. 3:16)

The Spirit that people receive from God within their bodies and minds is the pledge of his limitless love for them.

The very fact that people cry out to God in prayer is a sign that God's Spirit is in them. To address God as "Father" is a sign that God has made people his sons and daughters, and given them his own life. "And because you are his children, God has sent the Spirit of his Son into our hearts, crying, 'Abba! Father!' " (Gal. 4:6)

ALIVE WITH DIVINE LIFE

Paul never seems to tire of telling people that they are alive with divine life—if only they would recognize it! Time after time he reminds believers that the Spirit lives and acts in them.

The Old Testament says that when Moses returned from his forty-day mountaintop visit with God, his face glittered and glowed. His face shone so powerfully that the Israelites couldn't look directly at him without shielding their eyes. When Moses realized that he was alive with God's life, it burst forth for all to see. He had beheld the glory of the Lord and it was reflected in his face.

When people turn to the Lord and realize that God's Spirit is alive in them, they will be transformed like Moses. They will discover that they are fully alive and free, because "where the Spirit of the Lord is, there is freedom." (2 Cor. 3:17)

Spiritual transformation is not something that will happen only in heaven. It is happening now. "And all of us," cries Paul, "beholding the glory of the Lord, are being changed into his likeness from one degree of glory to another." (2 Cor. 3:18) And, he adds, this transformation comes from the Spirit.

10

*T*HE SPIRIT AND THE SACRAMENTS

THE SPIRIT AT WORK

The Holy Spirit is more than a mere footnote in human history. He is the shaper of that history. For the Spirit's work is to build up the total body of Christ—the greatest historical project of all.

If the Spirit is not recognized as important, it is because his work is hidden. It happens deep within people.

Some seem to notice only the things people do. They seem to see only *people* acting—and people are acting! But there is more. The Spirit within is also acting in them and through them.

Those who have learned to see human activity with Jesus-eyes are able to recognize the Spirit at work all around.

Life in the total body of Christ, which some people call "heaven," is already beginning to be made real in people. Everything that will be is somehow here now, slowly being transformed by the Spirit.

BUILDING THE KINGDOM

From the inside, the Spirit is building the community of believers into one grand Body. The Spirit wishes to preserve all individuals with all their skills and talents, so that each can live the life of the Body in as many ways as possible.

Each person *is* potentially the kingdom of God, for the Spirit is ready to become fully alive in them. "You are in the Spirit, since the Spirit of God dwells in you." (Romans 8:9)

As a group, humanity is also the kingdom of God for the Spirit is as fully alive in the whole as in the parts of the Total Body. Like individual cells in an organism, each cell is fully alive with its own unique life, and yet all the cells together form an organism which is fully alive with its own unique life.

The cells cannot survive alone without sharing the life of the organism, and the organism cannot live if there are no cells. Each believer shares the life of the community, yet the community cannot live if there are no believers.

What vivifies the Total Christ Body is the life of the Spirit. Anyone who belongs to the Christ Body has the Spirit of Christ. "For all who are led by the Spirit of God are sons and daughters of God." (Romans 8:14)

EXPRESSIONS OF THE TOTAL CHRIST

The Spirit performs his work in people informally, but he also acts formally through the Church. He does this principally in and through the sacraments.

Like spiritual milestones, sacraments mark important

stages in a believer's life. They commemorate different ways the Spirit acts in people who belong to the Church.

Sacraments are unique expressions of the Total Christ because they connect the organization-church with the community-church. Thus, while each sacrament finds a place in the formal organizational structure of the church, each contributes something special to the informal community of believers.

In every sacrament Jesus continues to send his Spirit.

Baptism

WELCOME TO THE TOTAL CHRIST

In baptism, a person is formally welcomed into the community of believers in Jesus.

The physical actions—pouring water on the skin, anointing with oil, pronouncing the baptismal formula —publicly affirm that the Church is enriched by a new person.

The organizational Church requires visible actions to publicly signify that a person is newly enrolled in its membership.

A baptismal certificate indicates formal membership in the Christian Church. It marks the first step, and allows the person to say such things as, "I belong to the Church. I am on record. I am registered. I publicly affirm my position as a member of this Church."

The living community, the informal structure of the Church, also affirms certain things in baptism. The baptized person is welcomed into a certain local community of believers.

COMMUNITY AFFIRMATIONS

Some of the affirmations made by the community in the baptism experience include the following. Believers may say to the newly baptized:

In Baptism

- You are welcomed into the Total Christ Body.

- You participate in the life of everyone here.

- You are washed in the same water as all of us—announcing the new kingdom.

- You are marked in the same way—with the sign of the cross —as all of us.

- You are like a grain of mustard seed which can grow into a tree.

- You are uniquely important in our community of love— there will never be another you.

In baptism, the Spirit helps believers put on the mind of Christ so that they now no longer see the world as merely a world. They now see it as Christ's Body.

A COMMON QUESTION

Some people may ask: "Why baptize a mere child? Why not wait until children have grown and may choose baptism themselves?"

One reason grownups baptize a child is because their action signifies welcoming the child into their community of love. Just as parents would never hesitate to welcome a newborn child into their home (their life, their community) as soon as possible, so believers would never hesitate to welcome a child into their Church (their Spirit life, their community) as soon as possible. The highest sign of love Christians can show to their children is to welcome them into the life of the Total Christ.

Confirmation

SERVING THE COMMUNITY

While baptism reassures people that they belong to the community, the sacrament of confirmation puts believers in touch with the community's work and service.

The physical actions of confirmation—such as standing before the community and being anointed with oil—publicly affirm that the believers being confirmed have reached a level of religious responsibility in the community.

In the organized Church, confirmed believers may be asked to involve themselves in the work and service of the organization and of the community.

The sacrament allows the person to say, "I am a responsible member. I am publicly recognized as a mature believer. I am willing to be called upon for work and service."

COMMUNITY AFFIRMATIONS

The loving community also affirms certain things in this sacrament. For example, it says:

In Confirmation

- You are ready for work and service among us.
- You are filled with energy from the Spirit.

- You have been given gifts, talents, and skills to use in helping build the Total Body.

- You have been strengthened for times of suffering.

- You have been prepared for the possibility that others may reject you.

- You have been called to help build the Body's unity.

The Spirit energizes and strengthens believers. He reveals to them their gifts and capacities. The Spirit helps believers to withstand suffering and welcome growth pains. The Spirit reminds believers that they are called to cooperate with him in building the Total Love Body.

In confirmation, believers put on the strength of Christ. By the Spirit, they are set free to act in the world with a new purpose—namely, to bring to its fullest stature the Total Christ.

Penance

UNCONDITIONAL ACCEPTANCE

In the sacrament of penance, or reconciliation, believers reaffirm God's unconditional acceptance of them. This experience encourages the basic response, "Let us *confess* that God is good."

Penance may be called the sacrament of inner healing, where each member is reconciled to all others in the community. Inner healing also symbolizes the importance of outer healing, from disease and anxiety.

The organizational Church acknowledges that believers sometimes publicly act in ways that contradict their baptismal membership. Sometimes these actions so strongly hinder the community's growth that the organization must require confession of them and contrition. In the sacrament of penance, the official Church offers ways for reconciliation to occur formally and publicly.

The physical acts in penance—the words of forgiveness, the healing touch—publicly affirm the believer's reacceptance by the organization.

The sacrament of penance allows a believer to say, "I am reinstated in the Church. Once more, I reaffirm my membership in good standing in the Church. I am reconciled with God and with the community."

COMMUNITY AFFIRMATIONS

The loving community also makes certain affirmations in the sacrament of penance. For example, it says:

In Penance

- Each of us is at the same time a good person and a sinner.
- Each of us personally needs God's loving mercy.
- Each of us is always reforming, growing.
- Each of us always needs ways of being reconciled to the community.
- Each one of us is called to be a reconciler—to show loving concern for one another.
- Each one of us is responsible for renewal and reform in the community.

In penance, the Spirit opens blocked channels of love and energy. Through each of us, the Spirit's healing power reaches everyone in the Body.

In penance, believers celebrate God's loving kindness to

them. Penance is a good-news experience, a healing experience.

In penance, believers celebrate the good news in the world—that the Total Body may always heal its weak members, because it lives with the healing Spirit's life.

Eucharist

FOOD TO GROW

In the Eucharist, in eating the holy communion, believers acknowledge that their Church community needs nourishment to grow.

The physical actions of the sacrament—eating the sacred bread and drinking the sacred wine—proclaim publicly that the community shares the same life and purpose.

Holy communion is a central action of the Church. It is the sacrament most frequently repeated. It is at the nucleus of the community's worship.

Whoever eats the Eucharistic bread affirms full membership in the community. It allows the believer to say, "I claim fellowship with all other Christians. I affirm my desire to live with the life of Christ."

COMMUNITY AFFIRMATIONS

In the Eucharist, the living community also affirms certain things of its members. It says, for example:

In the Eucharist

• Eating the same bread and wine helps us grow into the same Body—the Total Christ.

- Each of us is nourished into the Body in unique ways.
- Each one of us nourishes each other—we are all Eucharist for one another, we give our lives for each other.
- Whatever nourishes life on any level is ultimately food for the Total Body.
- The Total Body will gradually become manifest to the community.
- For each of us to grow is for the Total Body to grow.

In holy communion, believers ingest the life and breath of Christ. Believers are transformed, individually and collectively, to live and move and act as a new being— the Christ being. They are growing into the Total Christ being shaped by the Spirit.

The Eucharist is also a primary healing sacrament since it nourishes members of the Body. Through eating the Eucharist, the Body strengthens itself to heal itself and overcome its weaknesses. In all these processes, the Spirit is at work shaping the Total Christ.

Matrimony

LOVING RELATIONSHIPS

The sacrament of matrimony asserts that loving relationships are essential to the life and growth of the believing community.

The physical actions in the sacrament—the mutual contract of the spouses publicly made and the physical act of love performed by the partners privately[1]—affirm that the Church is primarily a community, fostering love and unity on all levels of life.

[1] For Catholics, marriage becomes canonically indissoluble only when the marriage contract is consummated in the physical act of love.

In the eyes of the organizational Church, spouses in marriage publicly affirm their intention of becoming the nucleus of a new love-community within the believing community. In many cases, this new love-community will bring children into the world who will in turn become formal members of the Church.

Other members of the community may attend a public marriage ceremony. They come to promise support and encouragement to the new couple who are making a contract to begin a new loving center in the community. The Church encourages this mutual support formally in the formal wedding ceremony.

COMMUNITY AFFIRMATIONS

The community itself affirms certain beliefs about spouses and the marriage relationship. For example, it says:

In Matrimony

- Spouses share life together.

- Spouses share their bodies with each other.

- Through their union they bring about new life.

- Spouses invite children to share life with them (formally in baptism, informally in the family).

- Spouses nurture children in the Church community (formally in the eucharist and in penance, when necessary, informally in moral development).

- Spouses help develop children's gifts, preparing them for service (formally in confirmation, informally by seeing to their education).

In matrimony, spouses participate bodily in building community. They learn to see their bodies and lives together in a new unity—as one body.

The loving marriage-body becomes a reproductive cell in Love's Body. In the Spirit, spouses acknowledge that they are alive *as partners* in the Total Christ.

Orders

SPOKESMEN AND SPOKESWOMEN

The sacrament of orders provides spokesmen for the Church. Their task is to reaffirm each local community's commitment to cooperate with the Spirit in shaping Christ's Body.

The physical actions in the conferral of orders include the laying on of hands and the public mandate announced by the bishop to the assembled Church members. The actions signify that the Church is a visible organism with its own life and traditions which need to be carried on through history. Those receiving orders are publicly entrusted with preserving the community's legacy.

The organizational Church needs to clearly identify its spokespeople, those who are its "word," its "*logos,*" who publicly affirm its meaning and purpose in the world, who publicly affirm its connection to Christ and dependence on his Spirit.

COMMUNITY AFFIRMATIONS

The informal community also makes certain affirmations about those who receive orders in the Church. For example, it says:

In Orders

- Spokespeople focus their major nurturing efforts on the Body as a whole.

- Spokespeople keep in touch with the community's past, present, and future, (i.e., they give the community its perspective).

- Spokespeople proclaim each member's freedom in the Total Body.

- Spokespeople proclaim each member's inherent power to do all that Jesus can do.

- Spokespeople affirm God's unconditional love for each member.

- Spokespeople formulate the community's response to God in public worship.

In the Total Christ Body which the Spirit is creating, the role of the public spokesperson is important. It involves recalling and reaffirming the community's values and vision.

Believers learn to see that the total community is itself a priest offering a loving response to God. The community is a priest because it lives with the life of Christ. Christ's Body which is offered in sacrifice is also the community's Body.

The community makes its commitment to the Total Christ through the Spirit.

Anointing

HEALING ILL MEMBERS

The sacrament called "anointing of the sick" is for healing individual community members, especially in time of serious illness.

The sacrament's physical actions—a community leader anoints the ill person with holy oils—publicly affirm that the human body is always important to the Church, even in illness and death.

In this sacrament, the organization Church affirms that it is concerned about the welfare of its members, especially when they are sick or dying.

This sacrament allows believers to say such things as, "I am cared for by the Church whenever I am seriously ill. My body and its health is important to the believing community."

COMMUNITY AFFIRMATIONS

The informal community also makes certain affirmations about anointing of the sick. For example, it may say:

In Anointing of the Sick

- Each believer's body is important and valuable.

- Believers depend upon each other for life and health.

- Community leaders lovingly touch sick member's bodies to affirm the bodily unity of the whole community.

- Believers live AND die on behalf of each other—that everyone may live in the Total Christ.

- Because of the community's love for each member, no member ultimately dies.

The sacrament of anointing also affirms that the Body never ultimately ceases to exist. Because believers live with the Spirit's life, they never die. Instead, they pass through death into fuller life in the Christ Body.

In anointing, believers acknowledge that all members share the same life, and all pass through the same gateway to life, because the Spirit operates within all, setting free the divine power within all.

THE UNBOUND SPIRIT

Whether in birth or death, whether eating or drinking, in loving or working, in proclaiming or being reconciled, the Spirit is at work in the Church, formally and informally, building up the community of believers. Whether visibly and publicly in the organizational Church, or invisibly and secretly in the hearts of the community, the Spirit is igniting the divine life in believers through the sacraments.

Although the Spirit has no need of sacraments to accomplish his purpose, yet he chooses to act through the formal Church and its sacraments to build up the Total Christ.

It is important to remember that the Spirit is not bound in any way by a formal organizational Church. He is at work in the entire world.

Believers and nonbelievers alike receive his love, since Christ's mandate to the Spirit involves leading the entire world back to God, to transform it totally, to infuse the whole universe with grace, to make all creation alive with God's life.

Three

THE SPIRIT
IN THE WORLD

11

Everywhere in the World

AT WORK IN PEOPLE AND EVENTS

Even after discussing the Spirit's influence in the sacraments and other activities of the Church, believers have only scratched the surface of the Spirit's activity. For there are many people and things in this world being transformed by the Spirit that will probably never be contacted by the Church in any formal way.

If the Spirit's activity were restricted to the Church alone, much of the world would remain Spirit-less. But, the truth is that the Spirit can be seen at work everywhere— in homes, factories, classrooms, offices, cars, busses, airplanes. He is in the world making everything new, ready at every place to rush in transforming things with his love.

Believers can select any person or event, no matter how insignificant or how seemingly evil, and see the Spirit at work there, somehow. Sometimes he is healing wounds, sometimes he is reconciling people to each other, sometimes he sets free feelings of joy and enthusiasm, sometimes he engenders hope or perseverance in a project.

In a very real sense, everything happening in the world that has to do with love, unity, freedom, truth, hope, joy, and the like is the work of the Spirit.

Look around to see how frequently the Spirit is at work in people and events. If people are curious to recognize the Spirit's work, that's a sign that they are inviting him to begin working in them. "He that has eyes to see, let him see," was the way Jesus put it.

THE POWER WITHIN

In the world, the Spirit reveals people's capacities and gifts, enables them to be patient and forgiving, cooperates with them in healing bodies and minds. The Spirit is the Power Within.

It cannot be stressed enough that the Spirit is at work everywhere in the world. No Church has a monopoly on the Spirit. No one can claim the Spirit as exclusively their own. The Spirit is essentially life, unity, love, freedom. Therefore, he will not be bound by any person, event, time, or place.

LIMITING THE SPIRIT

Sins against the Spirit include the refusal to allow the Spirit to work wherever he wills. For example, it offends the Spirit to say that the Spirit only works in *our* Church, or that the Spirit only works in *our* way, or that the Spirit only comes to *our* people.

Much human sinfulness springs from people setting boundaries or limits on the Spirit. In denying his pervasive presence, people deny the power within them to pray, heal, and accomplish good things in the world.

Those who deny that everyone is invited to live with God's life are limiting the Spirit.

Those who deny that people have the power to positively transform the world are limiting the Spirit.

Those who deny that certain people can become fully alive and hopeful are limiting the Spirit.

People cleverly invent many ways to block the Spirit's power from influencing themselves. They protect themselves from his activity by prejudices, biases, denials, obsessions, and the like. They may say things such as, "God can't love me" or "I'll never turn out to be any good" or "I'm just a puny nothing on this planet" or "The Spirit only works in those who attend Church."

How sad to see people bind and tie themselves in negatives.

Since the Spirit is blocked by negatives, people need to use a positive approach to set free the power within them. Rather than "I can't . . ." or "I'll never . . ." they can begin believing and say, "With his help, I can try" or "I'm just beginning to . . ."

LEARNING TO LISTEN

How can people begin to recognize the blocks they place in the Spirit's way? How can people open themselves so that the Spirit can help them become "all that Christ wants me to be"?

Listening is the key.

Learn to listen to *yourself* first. What is it you are saying in your inner dialogue?

Listen for your feelings. Listen for the times when the fire of enthusiasm begins to burn, and you quench the flame with a denial or bias. "It's silly for me to try that. It will never work."

Listen for the times when your heart wants to sing. Notice the times you cut off these and other good things when they were about to happen.

Listen for the urgings inside you. Listen for the curiosity that wants to search. Listen for the insights that want to surface.

ON THE ROAD

On the first Easter, two disciples on the road to Emmaus were talking to Jesus himself, the very person they so much wished was alive. Yet, by their denials and prejudices and limiting beliefs, they refused to let their eyes see Jesus who was walking alongside them. How effectively they suppressed the Spirit within them!

Only later on were they able to "listen" to what had happened within them. "Were not our hearts burning while we talked with him on the road?" (Luke 24:32)

How often the Spirit tries to break through into people's awareness, but he meets only blocks. People swear they do not block the Spirit, yet they often do.

12

$\mathcal{P}$RAYER

LISTENING TO THE SPIRIT

Prayer involves listening to the Spirit speaking within.

Prayer involves seeing the true picture of the world, the most complete picture. It involves being open to see things the way they are.

Ideally, prayer involves seeing people's lives and the world with God's eyes and hearing with his ears. This divine way of seeing and hearing is done with the Spirit —the Power Within.

People have defined prayer as "lifting the mind and heart to God." This definition seems to be another way of saying "putting on the eyes and ears of God."

When people put on God's eyes and ears, they can begin to see and listen to the Spirit at work.

INSIDE AND OUTSIDE

The Spirit operates both inside and outside the person who prays.

The Spirit facilitates prayer within the person, since it is only in the Spirit that people pray at all. "No one can say, 'Jesus is Lord' except in the Holy Spirit." (1 Cor. 12:3)

The effect of the Spirit within is especially clear when people find it difficult to pray. The Spirit himself takes over, and people find themselves praying despite themselves. "The Spirit helps us in our weakness, for we do not know how to pray as we ought; but the Spirit himself intercedes for us with sighs too deep for words." (Rom. 8:26)

The Spirit operates outside the believer, too.

Often, the subject matter of prayer, the focus of concern, usually involves the Spirit at work in people and events. People may pray for justice among men, peace among nations, and joy for the world. In each case, they are praying that the Spirit will bring about the kingdom of God. "The kingdom of God is . . . justice, peace and joy that is given by the Holy Spirit." (Rom. 14:17)

If individuals pray for their own sanctification, it is the work of the Holy Spirit.

If they pray for the salvation of others, it is the work of the Spirit.

If they pray that the world itself be transformed, that too is the work of the Spirit.

Believers who understand the all-pervasiveness of the Spirit realize that they and their concerns are never "on the outside" of the Spirit. The same Spirit that urges them to pray for something to happen is also at work *in the something* helping to make it happen.

Reflective Prayer

RE-CREATING THE GOSPEL

Reflecting in the Spirit is a very common form of prayer. In reflective prayer, believers read, for example, the New Testament story of the passion, death, and resurrection of Jesus, and in a prayerful mood reflect on what they read.

While reading, they may ask themselves, for example: What is the Spirit saying to us here and now in these words? What does the Spirit offer us in the way of "good news," "hope," or "faith?" What does the Spirit suggest to us about ways of behaving?

The struggle to answer such questions demands contact with the Spirit within.

The Christian community, or individuals in it, strive to recognize the gospel story in their own lives. They search for ways the Spirit is leading them, as he did Jesus, through their own passion, death, and rebirth. In formulating their experience from this viewpoint, they relive the paschal story. They re-create the gospel.

For such believers, "the gospel is not a dead letter," writes Juan Luis Segundo in *The Sacraments Today.* "It is a word which is incarnated again and again in different situations, different cultures, and different civilizations."

MY STORY

In this way, the gospel is "translated" again and again. The "good news" is now no longer merely the Jesus story, but *my story.*

Just as Jesus' story was the work of the Spirit, so every

believer's story is also the work of the Spirit. It deserves to be told and celebrated. Believers no longer need only speak of what the Spirit has done in Jesus' life, they may also announce what the Spirit has done in their lives.

On Pentecost morning, Peter and the apostles rushed from the upper room into the streets of Jerusalem, not merely to tell the story of Jesus. Peter's first words were to tell *what happened to him and the other disciples.*

"These men are not drunk," explained Peter. "This is what was spoken of by the prophet Joel: 'And in the last days, God declares, it shall be that I will pour out my Spirit upon all flesh . . .' " (Acts 2:15–17)

In reflective prayer, people may read the scriptures as if they were a pattern of how the Spirit works in them. When they read, they may ask questions like: "And where is *my* blindness that the Spirit wants to cure?" "Who are the people who wait to hear *my* voice of acceptance and concern?" "How is the Spirit urging *me* to pray to the Father?"

Instead of merely "consuming" the gospel, the Spirit invites people to "re-create" it, and after re-creating it, to celebrate it. "Be filled with the Spirit . . . sing praise to the Lord with all your hearts. Give thanks to God the Father always and for everything in the name of our Lord Jesus Christ." (Eph. 5:18–20)

Experiential Prayer

TOUCHED BY GOD

Reflective prayer leads to experiential prayer, which is also the work of the Spirit. Experiential prayer refers to activity of the Spirit experienced at the personal level.

Some may sense a divine presence within them when they pray alone. Others may experience God's love for them especially in a worship service. Still others may find new spiritual energies in them today to deal with a problem that seemed overwhelming yesterday. Experiential prayer refers to people having concrete knowledge of God. They somehow *feel* God in their lives.

Experiential prayer contrasts with abstract knowledge about God gained through reason, logic, and other forms of thinking. Experience refers to knowledge at the personal level: it touches *my* body, *my* mind, and *my* heart. It is *my* experience.

Experiential prayer, too, is meant to be shared with other people, for it inspires them. Hearing the work of the Spirit in one person's life opens others to the Spirit, so that the effects of the Spirit may be multiplied.

SEE HOW THEY LOVE EACH OTHER

For many early Christians, the Spirit was a living experienced fact. They recognized his activity in their daily lives and talked about it to others.

Such religious experience naturally flowed into their mission. Their "experiential prayer" manifested itself in faith and love. "See how they love each other," said people of early Christians.

Being in touch with the Spirit, they were often able to accomplish things beyond their natural capabilities. Witness the healings and miracles performed by the apostles.

Such extraordinary workings of the Spirit intensified the community's entire prayer life and often spontaneously produced prayers of praise. "Let us confess that God is good." (Ps. 118:1)

PRAYERS OF PRAISE

Frequently, experiential prayers are brought to a close in prayers of praise and thanksgiving. Such prayers are common in the psalms.

Many people find the prayer of praise feels unnatural to them, even forced. And it *is* when it does not happen as an overflow of religious experience.

Those in touch with the Spirit at work in their own life find praise a natural and spontaneous commentary on their experience. For them, praise is fitting. At meetings, pentecostal Christians commonly use prayers of praise.

As a result of experiential prayer, many believers experience the Spirit in their lives as a power for growth.

Some may grasp the Spirit's power, in order to uncover in themselves new levels of personal maturity; consequently, they may learn to relate to others in new ways or develop a capacity to know, to love, to care.

Others definitely experience new levels of Christ-awareness; they may feel the Spirit's life growing in them. Paul expressed this feeling in words: "I live—now, no longer I, but Christ lives in me." (Gal. 2:20)

Non-Conceptual Prayer

MESSAGES OF GOD

Joan of Arc, saint and mystic, often reported hearing voices that came from God. When Inquisitors at her trial told her the voices were only in her imagination, she replied, "Of course."

But she added perceptively, "That is how the messages of God come to us."

Non-conceptual prayer may be described as a form of spontaneous experiential prayer which often involves symbols and non-rational expressions. Non-conceptual prayer tends to involve non-ordinary mind levels. It utilizes creative imagination rather than reasoning.

Mystics and contemplatives are familiar with such prayer. More and more people today, especially among pentecostals, are reporting prayer experiences on these nonordinary mind levels.

In such situations, believers are found to be in nonordinary states of consciousness, where reason and logic are of little importance. These states are akin to the mind states in which mystical experience occurs. They are ecstatic in the sense that believers are taken *ex-stasis,* that is, out of their usual place!

Non-conceptual prayer experiences, usually occurring privately and spontaneously, include things like prophecy, visions, revelations, inspirations, locutions, speaking in tongues, levitation, dancing before the Lord, and so on. Many people have some experiences like these at various times in their lives.

The believer may experience non-conceptual states in a variety of ways: in interior imagery (as in visions or revelations), in messages heard interiorly (as in locutions or inspirations), in intuitive predictions (as in clairvoyance or prophecy), in spoken language, often unintelligible (as in tongues or singing), in spontaneous body movement (as in dancing or levitation). These are some non-conceptual ways the Spirit bursts forth in people.

GIFTS OF THE SPIRIT

Ecstatic experiences are recognized as gifts of the Spirit. For example, among believers speaking in tongues usually occurs as a prayer of praise. "The gift of the Holy

Spirit had been poured out even on the Gentiles, for they heard them speaking in tongues and extolling God." (Acts 10:46)

Prophecy, so essential to the building of the Total Christ, is a gift given to help the Church's mission. "And they were filled with the Holy Spirit and spoke the word of God with boldness." (Acts 4:31)

Spontaneous non-conceptual prayer was characteristic of the early Church. In recent centuries, however, the Church has stressed—perhaps overstressed—rational cognitive prayer.

Today's pentecostal Christians are reintroducing spontaneous non-conceptual prayer into the Church's life.

Once again, believers may feel free to sing and dance and shout before the Lord, as the Spirit moves them.

King David was a pentecostal before his time; he sang and danced before the Lord. (See 2 Kings 6:14)

Petition Prayer

IN ACCORDANCE WITH GOD

The prayer of petition—asking favors from God—is the prayer form most familiar to Christians.

"Ask and you shall receive, knock and it shall be opened to you." (Matt. 7:7)

"Whatever you ask the Father in my name, he will give to you. Hitherto you have not asked." (John 16:24)

In petition, the first rule is to pray in accordance with "God's will." That will is written into God's nature, which is love. So, when believers pray in accordance with the law of love, they pray in accordance with the will of God.

In a similar way, God's nature also follows the laws of truth, justice, unity, goodness. So whenever believers pray in accordance with the law of love, they pray in accordance with the will of God.

In a similar way, God's nature also follows the laws of truth, justice, unity, goodness. So whenever believers pray in accordance with the laws of justice, truth, unity, goodness, they pray in accordance with the will of God.

But all these qualities—love, justice, unity, truth, and the like—are gifts of the Spirit!

Because prayer of petition is so closely connected with the Spirit's work, pentecostal believers frequently ask for things from God. They pray for little things, they pray for big things. In their petitions, they count on the Lord to hear and grant them.

A PRAYER EXPERIMENT

In her book, *The Healing Light,* Agnes Sanford suggests an experiment for those who have not yet explored the power of petition prayer:

One decides upon a definite subject for prayer, prays about it, and then decides whether or not the prayer-project succeeds. If it does not succeed, one seeks a better adjustment with God and tries again.[1]

In order to see if the prayer experiment works, she says, decide on some tangible thing to pray for. Don't perform the prayer experiment on vague and indefinite requests such as, "peace in the world" or "a happy marriage" or

[1] *The Healing Light,* Charisma edition, 1972, p. 5.

"the salvation of my soul" or "repose of a deceased person." Instead, designate a specific and concrete outcome, such as, "that I won't get angry at my spouse tonight" or "that my child will be well and back to school by Wednesday" or "that I will feel more peaceful tomorrow than I do today."

In this way, you will know without question whether the experiment has succeeded or failed.

IF IT DOESN'T WORK

When prayer experiments fail, it is not the fault of the Spirit, for the Spirit's power, like electricity in the wires, is always available. It is most probably "a natural and understandable lack in ourselves," something we have failed to do.

If people switch on an electric light and it does not light, they don't say, "There is no electricity." Instead, they say, "Something's wrong with the lamp or the wiring."

After failing to receive a petition, prayer experimenters may be tempted to say, "There is no divine power."

Rather than give up, a true experimenter will try different ways to improve the lamp or repair the wiring until the current flows freely and the lamp lights.

When prayer seems to fail, a more helpful response might be, "Something's wrong in me or in my connections with the Spirit."

Thomas Edison, inventor of the electric light bulb, is said to have tried over six thousand different kinds of filaments before he found one that would contain electricity and create a glow for seeing.

A wise scientist studies the laws of science and adapts his experiments to those laws. A wise pray-er will study the laws of God—love, justice, truth—and adapt prayers to those laws.

13

$\mathcal{H}$EALING

EVERY DISEASE AND INFIRMITY

One of the simplest and most direct prayer projects involves healing of the body.

From the many healing stories in the New Testament, it is clear that for Jesus healing of bodily illness was a primary focus. Among all of Jesus' miracles, healing was the most frequent.

Healing and preaching the gospel were the two sides of his work. "And Jesus went about all the cities and villages, teaching in their synagogues . . . and healing every disease and every infirmity." (Matt. 9:35) Healings were signs that in Jesus, God's work was being done, that the power of God's spirit was in his preaching.

When Jesus gave his disciples their commission, he commanded them to do as he had done.

Their first commission was to heal. "Heal the sick, raise the dead, cleanse lepers, cast out demons." (Matt. 10:8)

The commission to preach the gospel includes power to heal the sick. "Whenever you enter a town and they receive you . . . heal the sick in it and say to them, 'the kingdom of God has come near to you.' " (Luke 10:8, 9)

So they went and did as Jesus had said. When they returned, they shared stories of healings they had done.

After Jesus' resurrection, his followers continued to effect healings. People carried their sick out into the streets and laid them on beds and pallets, "that as Peter came by at least his shadow might fall on some of them." (Acts 5:15) "Many who were paralyzed or lame were healed." (Acts 8:7) Even after the first apostles had died, healing continued to be evidenced in the life of the Christian community.

KINDS OF HEALING

Christian healing prayers differ with different kinds of sickness. There are three or four basic kinds of sickness that require healing.

The first is *sickness of the soul or spirit* caused by personal sin; it requires the prayer of *repentance* for healing.

A second is *emotional sickness,* for example, anxiety, depression, or excessive fear, caused by emotional hurts of the past; it requires a prayer for *inner healing,* or what some charismatics call "healing of memories."

A third is *physical sickness* in the body, caused by disease or accidents or an emotional problem; it requires *prayer for physical healing.*

Some would also list a fourth area where healing is needed. This area includes problems—they can be spiritual, emotional, or physical—brought about by *demonic influence;* these require the *prayer of deliverance* (sometimes exorcism).

Pentecostal believers today wish to renew the ministry of healing in the world. For them, healing involves both physical and interior healing. Like Jesus, they esteem interior healing and often view physical healing as a sign of interior renewal.

SCIENCE AND SPIRIT

Pentecostal believers are not opposed to medical or psychiatric care. Rather, scientific healing techniques are valued. Since the Spirit works primarily according to the laws of nature, every attempt is made to utilize available natural gifts and skills to effect bodily and mental healing.

At the same time, prayers for healing and the laying on of hands indicate that the healing process, natural or supernatural, is the Spirit's work.

The Spirit works to heal through doctors, counselors, nurses, and the like, as well as through prayers for healing. Physicians, psychotherapists, nurses, parents are all ministers of healing, inspired by the Spirit.

It is a false dichotomy to set up physicians and other scientific professionals as "secular healers" and Christian prayer people as "sacred healers." According to Reverend Francis MacNutt, "All these different professions with their different competencies go to make up God's healing team."[1]

HEALING AND SUFFERING

The pentecostal renewal of healing does not dismiss the mystery of suffering.

For some people, suffering can be a purifying and re-

[1]From an address reprinted in *New Covenant,* March 1974, p. 30.

demptive experience. It may be designed by the Spirit to effect an interior transformation that might otherwise never happen.

However, the Spirit is primarily working toward the health of the Christ Body. And, whenever there is the slightest question about suffering, we may presume that the Spirit is working toward physical and interior health, that is, to relieve the suffering.

This, too, is clearly the mentality of Jesus, for nowhere in the New Testament does Jesus, when faced with someone desiring to be healed, say anything like, "No, I won't heal you. It's better for you that you suffer."

The only case of suffering Jesus condoned was his own, in his passion and death. Yet, even in the garden at Gethsemane Jesus was not sure that his suffering was fitting. In fact, Jesus did not seem to want it. He asked, "Father, if you are willing, remove this cup of suffering from me." (Luke 22:42)

Many people resign themselves—and others!—to suffering, without ever questioning whether this suffering is willed by God.

HEALTH IN THE TOTAL CHRIST

It seems more in line with Jesus' mentality to struggle against physical illness and interior discontent, wherever they occur. God's will for humans is health and unity. The Spirit's work is to bring about ever greater health and unity.

Whenever illness proves destructive or produces chaos, let people wrestle against it with the Spirit as their partner. Accept suffering only when God's will seems irrefutably to indicate it.

During his life, Jesus struggled against suffering brought about by injustice, hate, and illness. He used his own powers and skills in connection with the Spirit.

In today's world, people can become other Christs using their powers and gifts in partnership with the Spirit in bringing about justice, love, and health in the Total Christ.

14

IFTS

CONCERNED WITH GIFTS

Certain groups of believers call themselves Charismatics because of their concern with the Spirit's charisms, that is, his gifts of power and service.

Charismatic believers are also sometimes called pentecostals because they view life in the Church community as a perpetual Pentecost; that is, they see the Spirit continually pouring out his power and gifts upon the people as he did on the first Pentecost.

In either case, whether they are called pentecostal or charismatic believers, they are concerned with the Spirit's gifts.

Although certain Christian groups may be concerned with spiritual gifts, no group has a monopoly on the Holy Spirit or his gifts. His presence and power is freely given to the entire Church, and also to the entire world.

FREE GIFTS

The Spirit comes to the Church community as a gift-giver. And his gifts are free.

The Spirit himself is his first gift to the Church.

The Spirit's charisms—love, joy, peace, wisdom, prophecy, tongues, and the like—are also his gifts to the Church.

They have been given to the Church *as gifts.* They belong to the Church in the same way that a gift "belongs" to a person. In gift giving, the giver usually remains free to give similar gifts to others. Thus, if a wealthy uncle gave a thousand dollars to one nephew, he is still free to give a thousand dollars to other nephews or nieces—or to anybody else, for that matter.

This seems very clearly to be the way the Spirit disperses his gifts throughout the world. Among Buddhists, Hebrews, and Mohammedans, among atheists and agnostics, the Spirit is clearly at work bringing love, peace, joy, and the rest. So, it is a limiting way of thinking about the Spirit to say that he and his gifts belong *only* to the Christian Church.

It is even more incorrect theologically to say that the Spirit and his gifts belong to a particular group within the Christian Church, such as the pentecostals or charismatics.

In the Church there are no special classes of Spirit-bearers, no isolated groups of Spirit-filled believers. To say otherwise is to deny the work of the Spirit—which is to unify the one body of Christ. To limit the Spirit in this way would be to work against his purpose.

More accurately, everyone is invited to participate in the Spirit. His gifts may be viewed as a common possession by the whole believing community.

However, when believers fail to realize opportunities offered by the Spirit, pentecostal Christians may become influential and important. By their activity, they highlight the presence and power of the Spirit in our world for those who may have forgotten it.

SPECIAL ROLE OF PENTECOSTAL CHRISTIANS

The special Spirit-related experiences described in the New Testament, say pentecostal Christians, can also happen in the same way in our time. Pentecostals believe people today can have direct contact with the Spirit just as the apostles did. And they find themselves experiencing the Spirit in visions, healings, prophecy, tongues, and in dealing with the demonic.

Some people have accused pentecostals of making exclusive claim on the Spirit and his gifts. Quite the opposite. Their purpose, like the apostles', is to invite all believers to realize the Spirit and his gifts *in themselves.*

They would assert that *every Christian is meant to be a charismatic.*

The Spirit and his gifts belong to the Christian community, since it is essentially a community of service—service to each other and to the world. To call oneself a Christian is already a commitment to the Total Christ. It is to say:

I am not a passive member of the community. I recognize the need to bring about love and justice in the world, and I am here to serve. I have been given gifts by the Holy Spirit to be used for the community.

As Paul expressed it: "To each is given the manifestation of the Spirit for the common good." (1 Cor. 12:4–7)

"In this sense," writes theologian Kilian McDonnell, "every Christian is a charismatic and therefore has a ministry to the Church and world."[1]

ANONYMOUS CHRISTIANS

Even in the earliest days of the Church, the Spirit spread his power wherever he wished. He worked independently of baptism and independently of the apostles. In their travels, the apostles sometimes came upon unbaptized nonbelievers who had obviously received the Spirit. (See Acts 10:44–48)

The Spirit often turned people into "Christians" before they had heard the "good news." And he still does.

For this reason, be careful not to use the label "Christian" in any narrow or restricted sense. There are many "anonymous Christians" walking our planet who may have never heard of Christ or his Church, yet are filled with the Spirit.

To receive the Spirit is to become a Christian, even if it is "anonymously." To be open to the influence of the Spirit is to live and act as Jesus did.

[1] *Theological and Pastoral Orientations on the Catholic Charismatic Renewal,* prepared at Malines, Belgium, May 21–26, 1974, text by Kilian McDonnell, © 1974 by Word of Life available from the Communication Center, P. O. Drawer A, Notre Dame, Indiana, 46556.

15

GIFTS AND SERVICE

GIFTS THAT ARE NEEDED

The Spirit's gifts are many. In a certain time and place, he gives whatever gifts are needed for building up the local community and the Total Christ.

The charisms or gifts of the Spirit are so many that it is simpler to say they are without number.

Or, more simply, each believer has his or her gifts from the Spirit to help cooperate in the work of the Spirit.

Christians have the responsibility to discover their gifts and to use them for developing the community and the Total Body.

Some tend to avoid this responsibility. One temptation is to say, "The Spirit's gifts are too high and exalted for me. I am not called to prophecy or to heal or to cast out demons." With words like these, some Christians might excuse themselves from discovering their gifts and serving the community with them.

DON'T PASS OVER "ORDINARY" GIFTS

Believers may best begin their search among the more ordinary gifts, for example, whatever encourages love, joy, patience, kindness, goodness, faithfulness.

Everyone has capacities to love, to be joyful, and so on. These are the Spirit's gifts to them.

In order to discover their particular gifts, believers need to ask themselves, "What loving abilities do I have? In what ways can I bring about joy in my family? How can I show patience and encourage it in others?" And so on.

"By their fruits you shall recognize them," said Jesus. But, "The fruit of the Spirit is love, joy, peace, patience, kindness, goodness, faithfulness, gentleness, and self control." (Gal. 5:22) Wherever there is kindness, goodness, and faithfulness, there is the Spirit.

How few people think of their ability to show love or joy or patience as a *gift of the Spirit.* Yet it is! Each of these abilities can bring about a sort of healing, or help to develop the loving community.

Everyone likes people who are loving or joyful or patient. They make life easier and richer for everybody. They help bring people together. Obviously, it is the Spirit at work.

WHERE TO LOOK FOR GIFTS

God has given gifts to each human. "Grace was given to each of us according to the measure of Christ's gift." (Eph. 4:7)

But how may someone discover the gifts God has given them? Paul answers: The Spirit helps us understand the gifts given us by God. (See 1 Cor. 2:12)

When searching for the Spirit's gifts in people's lives, don't overlook daily occupations.

Many contemporary gifts from the Spirit will not be listed in Paul's writings, since Paul was unfamiliar with much of today's scientific and technological language used to describe skills and talents.

Some current gifts might include being a biologist, a communications expert, a psychologist, a paleontologist, an ecologist, an electronics technician, an inventor, and so on. Discoveries in all these fields have made people more aware of human growth. They have helped humans become more aware of needs and necessities for building up the Body of Christ.

People's gifts may include very traditional ones, except that today they may have new names.

For example, one gift Paul listed was that of "teacher." In early Church times there were no colleges and universities as we understand them, nor newspapers or radio and television stations. And each of these places employ people who *teach* in one way or another.

Today under "teacher" Paul might have listed all who inform, explain, or communicate knowledge. His list would include professors, writers, researchers, reporters, script writers, announcers, editors, receptionists, and so on.

All of these "teacher" callings involve Spirit gifts that certainly help bring the One Body together. Shared knowledge and understanding is very important to loving unity.

Certain important gifts of the Spirit may be very obvious ones that Paul never bothered to mention. Some gifts usually taken for granted, gifts that almost everyone possesses, are discussed in the following pages.

GIFT OF LISTENER

The gift of *listener* has a wide variety of important uses. Modern psychiatry and counseling emphasize the therapeutic effects of listening. Friendships are made by listening. Family members often turn to each other for sympathy and understanding. Self-confidence and trust are built up in any relationship through listening.

Listeners usually also possess other fruits of the Spirit such as love, patience, peace, gentleness, understanding and self-control.

Listening is a cornerstone of a loving community. Blessed are those called by the Spirit to be listeners.

Listeners are also healers, especially when hurt has come from misunderstanding, jealousy, and the like. Rev. Eugene C. Kennedy writes in *A Time for Love:*

The Spirit makes it possible for lovers who have wounded each other to bring again a healing presence to each other. It means that we can make up for our smallness, our jealousies, and all our broken resolutions, not by a new and unrealistic pledge never to fall again, but by a willingness to take up the task of loving again. Real love begins when we are ready to forgive each other and help each other to do better the next time, not when we expect each other to go through life with all our lines letter-perfect.[1]

Listening is no "automatic skill," it needs to be learned and practiced. It is a gift like a talent for music. It does not excuse recipients from practicing in order to develop their gift.

Prophecy, a very special Spirit gift, involves listening. A prophet may be described as one who first *listens to God* and then proclaims the message that was heard.

[1]*A Time for Love,* Doubleday & Co., New York, 1970, p. 167.

GIFT OF CONNECTOR

Often overlooked is the gift of *connector,* the person who brings together those who need to be connected to each other. A connector says, for example, "You must meet so-and-so, why don't you both come over to my place for lunch tomorrow?" Or, "May I introduce so-and-so, you two have a lot in common."

Connectors whet interest in other people. They establish communication between people who might never otherwise meet. In many different ways, connectors knit the human community together in unity and harmony.

Jesus counted on connectors to introduce him to his disciples. John the Baptist connected John and Andrew with Jesus; Andrew connected him with Peter; Philip connected him with Nathaniel, and so on. Who can say that this is not the work of the Spirit?

Many individuals have been "putting the right people together" and probably never recognized their "connector" talent as a Spirit gift.

Many others, too, possess this ability but have never used it. Instead, like the last man in the parable of the talents, they buried their connector ability in the ground, where it waits to be resurrected.

Perhaps it is time for those who have buried their talents to have a treasure hunt! "The kingdom of heaven is within you," said Jesus.

GIFT OF PATRON

The gift of *patron* is another often forgotten gift. A patron is a person who, without jealousy or envy, welcomes gifts in others and promotes them.

History is full of wealthy people who did not personally possess talents—for painting, sculpture, music, science, drama, etc.—but *recognized these talents in others,* and provided ways for them to develop and be seen and heard.

Talented people, such as artists, inventors, scientists, and the like, have special needs: time to develop their art, money to survive financially, supplies to exercise their talents, and situations where their talents can be displayed. Patrons are people who help take care of such needs.

Think how many wonderful gifts—perhaps even in yourself—were never developed and recognized because there was no patron to comfort, support, encourage, and challenge them.

Today, many large corporations—the Lilly Fund, the Ford Foundation, and the like—act as patrons but their patronage is usually just financial.

Parents and other community leaders have many opportunities to notice people with special talents and encourage them.

Children need to know how to participate meaningfully in life, even if only in a small way. In his book, *Education and the Creative Potential,* Dr. E. Paul Torrance encourages Christian parents and teachers to help children live creatively:

We are taught that we were made "in the image and likeness of God," and when we create we are to some extent exercising that God-like quality within us. It gives us a feeling of contentment and satisfaction. To groups of educators, I have frequently asserted that the greatest reward a child achieves for learning, is doing something with what he has learned, using it to think and to behave creatively.[1]

[1] *Education and the Creative Potential,* The Modern School Practices Series—Number Five, The University of Minnesota Press, Minneapolis, 1963, p. 90.

Some famous people have become so only because one or more patrons helped them on the road to success.

Thomas Edison, inventor of the electric light bulb, the phonograph, and many more things, was laughed at as a child, but his mother never ceased encouraging him.

The Queen of Portugal was patron to Christopher Columbus; without her financial assistance and her belief in him, he would never have discovered America.

Michaelangelo, creator of world famous paintings and sculpture, was supported by the popes of his day.

"Do not put your light under a basket," said Jesus. Patrons help display people's lights where others can clearly see and enjoy them—and perhaps praise God because of them. Think of Michaelangelo's painting on the ceiling of the Sistine Chapel.

"Sometimes our light goes out," wrote Albert Schweitzer, "but is blown again into flame by an encounter with another human being. Each of us owes the deepest thanks to those who have rekindled this inner light."

Before an important decision he had to make, the famous statesman Dag Hammarskjöld was looking for some sign from God. That night he wrote in his diary about the sign he received:

> Before an important decision
> someone clutches your hand—
> a glimpse of gold in the iron-gray,
> the proof of all you have never dared to believe.[1]

GIFT OF ORGANIZER

A fourth forgotten gift, so desperately in demand nowadays, is that of *organizer* or *manager.*

[1] *Markings,* Alfred A. Knopf, New York, 1966, p. 61.

When large numbers of people need to be contacted and reached, it is not enough for people simply to be *willing* to do something. Many wheels must turn and many details must be taken care of before the curtain opens.

Organizers have a gift for remembering detail and keeping everything straight in their heads. Ask organizers of a catechetics workshop how many things they had to do or remember to tell others to do before the meetings got underway. Count the phone calls, the tickets, the printing, the arrangements, the purchase slips, the lists made and item-by-item taken care of, the complaints and suggestions listened to, finding the volunteers, scheduling the staff, making the posters, and so on.

Behind the scenes, the organizer takes care of all this so that the lights go on, the microphones work, the lecturers get transportation, and the people come—all at the right time.

In the Church, whenever good things happen in groups, there is probably someone gifted as organizer helping account for success. In picnics, card parties, potluck suppers, clubs, food campaigns, walk-a-thons, educational programs, sermon series, social action groups, conventions, conferences, and a thousand other Church activities, the Spirit is at work in organizers helping to unify the Total Body in every way possible.

GIFT OF FUND-RAISER

For some, fund-raiser may seem a distasteful gift. "I hate to beg," they may say. Fund-raising may seem less spiritual than other gifts.

Anyone knows that no organization, group, or family survives today without someone who can bring in money to support the group's activities. Churches, schools, hospitals, clubs, theaters, all groups need individuals who can communicate enthusiasm for a cause to those who might contribute to it.

The gospels make little mention of fund-raising in Jesus' ministry. But there are hints of wealthy contacts and generous friends. The group that traveled with Jesus probably tapped their friends' financial resources from time to time.

In the early Church, Paul was a fund-raiser. He often spoke to wealthier communities urging them to support the less well-to-do Christian Churches. He speaks of collections, sending money here and there, coming to collect it, and so on.

From the very first days of the Church, the Spirit was giving certain people the gift for "making ends meet."

GIFTS BENEFIT THE COMMUNITY

Any community develops its potential best and most effectively when its members recognize and use their gifts on behalf of the whole community.

People who realize their gifts and are open to the Spirit can never remain in their community only as recipients. Instead of only counting on others for their needs, they are impelled by the Spirit to activate their own gifts among people. In this way they contribute to the growth of the One Body.

Robert Kennedy, assassinated during the United States presidential campaign of 1964, made a commitment to use his talents for the common good. He is reported saying:

Sometimes it seems to me that it doesn't matter what I do, that it is enough to exist, to sit somewhere, in a garden for example, watching whatever is to be seen there, the small events.

At other times, I'm aware that other people, possibly a great number of other people, could be affected by what I do or fail to do, that I have a responsibility, as we all have, to make the best possible use of whatever talents I've been given, for the common good.

It is not enough to sit in that garden, however restful or pleasurable it might be. The world is full of unsolved problems, situations that demand careful, reasoned, and intelligent action.[1]

In exercising their gifts, people help bring forth new creations—in the world, in others, and in themselves.

In exercising their capacities, people are invited by the Spirit into the fulness of their own potential. Using gifts and talents is like making an investment which can multiply and bring profit to the investor.

Some people recognize and reverence the Spirit at work everywhere. Others never really "see" the flame of God burning before their eyes. Loving poet Elizabeth Barrett Browning described it this way:

> Earth's crammed with heaven
> And every common bush afire with God;
> And only he who sees takes off his shoes—
> The rest sit round it and pluck blackberries.

St. Francis of Assisi recognized the Spirit at work in "every common bush." In all the ordinary things of life, he knew God was touching him deeply. "Even if I knew the world were going to end tomorrow," Francis once said, "I would go out and plant apple trees today."

[1]Quoted in "Robert Kennedy Saved from Drowning,"
© 1968 by Donald Barthelme.

16

DISCOVERING AND USING GIFTS

DISCOVERING YOUR GIFTS

In any community, some people may not have discovered their gifts, while others may be aware of their gifts but have not yet begun to use them for the common good.

In such situations, the Spirit's usual strategy is to use people—leaders, moderators, and other members of a community—to evoke hidden and unused talents in others. Such evocative people may be called *enablers* of gifts.

How often others are first to recognize capacities in people of which they may be unaware!

WHEN GIFTS ARE SUPPRESSED

Perhaps the worst situation involves communities where people are denied opportunities to use and develop their gifts. This is especially true of minority groups, those in third world nations, the poor and hungry.

Imagine the transforming potential of all those people going to waste!

One of today's challenges to Christians is to find ways of uncovering gifts among socially and economically handicapped peoples.

Another challenge involves finding ways of helping such people creatively use their gifts. Listeners, connectors, patrons, organizers, fund-raisers, enablers are all needed for this work.

The Spirit needs to come alive in oppressed people everywhere, to break forth in spiritual fire, to release its power in them.

Rather than having so-called more powerful people "solve the problem of the oppressed," the Spirit seems to be suggesting another way: help make oppressed people aware of the *power within themselves to change the situation in which they presently live.*

"Building the earth" (Teilhard de Chardin's phrase) will come about when everyone discovers their own gifts and uses them creatively. When used, gifts carry people out among others and allow them to fully participate in life.

GIFTS AND GOD'S WILL

A person's gifts are clearly related to God's will for him or her.

Some individuals pray to know the will of God for them without suspecting that this will is already written into their very lives *as gifts.*

For someone to perceive their gifts is to perceive God's will.

Elizabeth O'Connor wrote a provocative book on gifts and creativity, titled *The Eighth Day of Creation.* She suggests that parents can easily observe gifts and talents that shine out in a child's life pointing the way to "God's will" for that child.

Every child's life gives forth hints and signs of the way that he is to go. The parent that knows how to meditate stores these hints and signs away and ponders over them. We are to treasure the intimations of the future that the life of every child gives to us so that, instead of unconsciously putting blocks in his way, we help him to fulfill his destiny. This is not an easy way to follow. Instead of telling our children what they should do and become, we must be humble before their wisdom, believing that in them and not in us is the secret that they need to discover.[1]

"A child of God who received the wisdom and the power of the Spirit," wrote Ladislas M. Örsy, S.J., "has a new capacity to see and a new capacity to love."[2]

In every human the creation story needs to be told anew. For the Spirit is continually recreating the Total Christ, and each one is invited to participate in it.

What a creative community the Church would be if it encouraged each person to "grow according to the design which is written into his being."[3]

Pentecostal Christians encourage the discovery and enjoyment of gifts. In this they are models for the entire Church community.

Each one is ultimately responsible for his or her own personal gifts.

People who do not use their gifts may experience anguish and frustration. Rather than fear of punishment for failing to discover and use gifts, most people would prefer to be shown *ways* to discover their potential. Procedures for discovering one's gifts are simple and direct.

---

[1] *The Eighth Day of Creation: Gifts and Creativity.* Word Books, Publisher, Waco, Texas, 1971, p. 18.
[2] *Open to the Spirit,* Corpus Books, Washington, D. C., 1968, p. 215.
[3] *Ibid.,* p. 17.

DISCOVERING AN INNER VOICE

People may listen to what the Spirit says within them.

The Spirit's voice does not sound like a stranger's voice. It is perhaps the most familiar voice people know—the one that speaks within them continually. Usually the inner voice makes requests for immediate needs. How often have people heard this voice say to them, "I think I need a break now," "I feel thirsty," "Can't wait to get home," "My favorite program will be on in five minutes," "I really need sleep," and so on.

That's an inner voice making its daily requests.

But that same inner voice, in moments of quiet and all-togetherness, also says things like, "That's something interesting to really study," "I don't find much meaning in my job," "She's somebody I really would like to know," "I'll bet I could do that if I tried," "That will take a lot of patience, but it'll be worth it." And so on.

Whenever such inner urgings would produce some little increment of peace, joy, love, wisdom, unity, and the like, they are probably the Spirit's inner urgings coming from the core of a person's being.

It takes time, physical time, for people to warm up enough to become sensitive to the invisible actions of the Holy Spirit. Theologian Ladislas M. Örsy writes:

Anyone who wants to communicate personally with God will have to direct his attentions to the Holy Spirit living in him. But the inspirations of the Spirit are always gentle and subtle; they require our *full* attention. Hence external noise should be excluded, internal worries should be calmed. When there is peace, the voice of the Spirit will be heard.[1]

[1] *Open to the Spirit,* Corpus Books, Washington, D. C., 1968, p. 244.

When people take the time to listen and ponder over their inner voice, they begin to discover *their way,* or as some would say, they begin to discover "God's will for them."

When people are faithful to their inner call—the gentle voice of the Spirit within—they experience meaning and purpose. They experience their gift as their own, and it fosters growth. Responded to, it brings a sense of wholeness, completeness, rightness.

Responding to an inner voice, accepting one's gifts and using them for the community, is self-confirming.

People need no one else to tell them, "This is right for you." If it's right, they know it. What others say—whether they encourage or discourage—in no way affects the rightness that they feel inside.

IDENTIFYING AND BLOCKING

Sometimes it takes a long time to identify the Spirit's gifts.

Some people are distracted by what others tell them to do, and some people may for years pursue an unsatisfying course.

People may block the Spirit's gifts in a variety of ways.

Some may prefer to be jealous or envious of another's gifts, and avoid admitting their own gifts.

Other people are tempted to reject their own gifts because they prefer to possess the gifts of another.

Many people also feel threatened or intimidated by another's gifts, and so won't use their own. Meeting obstacles along the way sometimes makes people begin to think that they were not called to work in this area and had better withdraw.

Fear of failure is another reason for not engaging in the use of gifts.

Others, entwined in timidity, may hesitate to really try out what they think are their gifts. They seldom if ever come to experience their gifts in a deeply satisfying way. They also avoid the risk of failure. Better to leave the gift buried somewhere, they may say, so that nobody else will know about it.

In his book *The Holy Spirit,* R. A. Torrey encouraged people to be open to the Spirit's gifts flowing through them, especially when the gifts seem stopped or blocked.

What is it that stops the fountain in your heart? Do you know? If so, put it away today. But perhaps you do not know what it is. You know you once had that joy and you know you have lost it. Well, you can know. Ask God to show you what it is that stops the fountain and promise Him that if He will show you what it is, you will give it up. He will show you if you are really sincere.[1]

One consolation for those who have not yet found their gifts, or ways to exercise them, is that the Spirit never ceases to remind them of their gifts. The Spirit knows their secret, no matter how deep down it is stored. Every secret wants to be discovered. It waits and will not remain buried forever.

OTHER WAYS TO DISCOVER GIFTS

Sometimes people discover their gift only in the exercise of their gift. This is not as paradoxical as it sounds.

Everyone has had the experience of recognizing gifts in others, before others recognize their own gifts. Recall the person with a delightful sense of humor who doesn't

[1] *The Holy Spirit,* Fleming H. Revell Company, 1927, p. 105.

realize it, the person who is a marvelous communicator on the telephone but doesn't know it, the person who is a natural actor or entertainer and is unaware of it, the person who is a born organizer but never suspected it.

In such cases, others may point out to such people their gifts *as they are being exercised.* They may say, "See how good you are on the phone," or "See how well you organized that party" or "See how you've managed to get everybody relaxed and laughing."

Such gifted people will recognize whether other's statements about them are correct or incorrect.

People need to encourage one another to discover and use the gifts that await expression in their deepest selves. Young people especially need encouragement to search out their gifts.

A community as a whole is accountable for the gifts of its members. This responsibility includes "naming" the gifts of each, offering opportunities for people to exercise their gifts, and encouraging and supporting people when they do exercise their gifts. Accepting gifts leads to commitment.

TRANSFORMING THE WORLD

Accepting and using the Spirit's gifts results in self-transformation and transformation of the community.

Always and everywhere, the Spirit is slowly and thoroughly bringing to reality the one great loving community which will one day recognize its own gift—that it is the Body of the Total Christ, the Body of the Jesus who is Lord.

The Spirit shines in those who are in communion with the Total Christ. St. Basil explains:

Just as brilliant and translucent bodies, penetrated by the rays of the sun, gleam with additional splendor and in their turn radiate a more intense brilliance, so those that are the temples of the Spirit are bathed in His light and become spiritual and radiate grace to others.[1]

Christians caught up in the Spirit's work express their longing for the Total Christ when they say, "Come, Lord Jesus."

Jesuit poet Gerard Manley Hopkins was able to see the world charged with the Spirit's life.

The world is charged with the grandeur of God.
    It will flame out, like shining from shook foil;
    It gathers to a greatness, like the ooze of oil
Crushed. Why do men then now not wreck his rod?
Generations have trod, have trod, have trod;
    And all is seared with trade; bleared, smeared with toil;
    And wears man's smudge and shares man's smell: the soil
Is bare now, nor can foot feel, being shod.

And for all this, nature is never spent;
    There lives the dearest freshness deep down things;
And though the last lights off the black West went
    Oh, morning, at the brown brink eastward, springs—
Because the Holy Ghost over the bent
    World broods with warm breast and with ah! bright
        wings.

[1]St. Basil, *De Spiritu Sancto,* IX, 22/23; P.G., XXXII, 109